Click. Trust. Regret.

A chilling reflection of the decision-making moments that lead to scams.

Acknowledgments

No one gets individual credit for any book ever written. This book has been written based on the support, guidance and contributions of many either given directly or indirectly. The aim has been largely to understand and combat the world of cyber scams even as technology gets more sophisticated.

To the cybersecurity community – The combatants of cyber threats as they evolve. Your relentless dedication to staying ahead of threats and educating the world inspires this work. Your insights and expertise have laid the foundation for the stories and lessons shared in this book.

To the victims of scams – Thank you for sharing your stories with courage and honesty. Your willingness to turn painful experiences into valuable lessons is a testament to your resilience.

To friends and family – Your encouragement and unwavering belief in this project made all the difference. Thank you for lending an ear, offering feedback, and reminding me why this work matters.

To the readers – This book exists because of you. Your commitment to learning, staying vigilant, and spreading awareness is the reason we can create a safer digital future.

Lastly, it would be unfair not to pay homage to the frontliners in the war against cyber threats in any form. Your unwavering efforts in protecting individuals and organizations from harm deserve greater accolades than words can say. This book is a tribute to your work and the impact you continue to make.

Together, we can turn knowledge into power and create a digital world where trust conquers fear.

Dedication

To everyone who aspires to a beautiful world, those who are dauntless in ensuring that we can make the world a better place that understand that awareness is the first step to protection, and knowledge is the greatest shield in the digital world.

Disclaimer

While this book speaks about the harsh realities of the internet and draws from stories of those who have fallen victims of different types of scams, all the names used in the book including organizations are purely fictitious as these people do not exist, should you meet someone with a similar name who has had similar experiences. Also, the book is not written to shame these people but to educate us all on the common threats we would usually come across on the internet on a daily basis.

Contents

Contents

Introduction
The Digital Wild West

It was just another normal day or so she thought. The email that would change the mood arrived in the evening, when Sarah thought she was wrapping up her day. Looking undoubtedly solid, with the bank's logo, an email with a familiar tone of urgency and a subject line designed to grab attention dropped in her inbox: "Unauthorized access detected. Act now to secure your account."

Sarah frowned. Could someone really have accessed her account? The sender's name looked right, and the message included a link that promised an immediate fix. With unhindered hesitation, her finger hovering over the mouse, unease chipping at her from the inside, she felt a wave of panic in a situation where the access was real, and someone actually had access to her account. What if her savings were at risk?

She clicked the link.

Miles away, Marcus was only picking up his mail and going through them when he noticed that his bank statement had transactions that he swore that he never made and couldn't recognize. His stomach tightened. He hadn't noticed anything unusual before, but now his statement showed that he had recorded large purchases and shockingly in Mexico, when he had not even left the United States in some years.

Sadly, what he was witnessing at the moment were the results of some clicks at different stages in his browsing history that allowed malicious people to piece information about him together and sell that to willing buyers on the dark web.

Two clicks. Two choices. Two lives forever changed.

The Invisible Enemy

These moments may sound like plot points from a thriller, but they're anything but fiction. Every day, people like Sarah and Marcus make decisions like these. Sometimes they hesitate, sometimes they trust their instincts, and sometimes; whether out of fear, urgency, or distraction; they act.

What they don't realize is that these moments are traps, meticulously set by cybercriminals who prey on our emotions, habits, and the fast pace of modern life. The outcomes aren't just measured in money lost but in confidence shattered.

Sarah and Mark aren't alone. Scammers are everywhere, lurking behind innocent-looking emails, friendly phone calls, and too-good-to-be-true offers. Their methods are as varied as the people they target, and their success depends on one simple thing: getting you to act before you think.

Why This Book Exists

In today's digital world, opportunities for communication, commerce, and information sharing abound. However, this vast landscape also presents significant risks, with cybercriminals constantly devising new and sophisticated ways to exploit unsuspecting individuals.

One of the most prevalent threats is phishing scams. According to a 2023 report by the Federal Trade Commission (FTC), consumers lost over $10 billion to various frauds in the previous year alone. Investment scams accounted for more than $4.6 billion of these losses, highlighting the growing danger of online deception.

Romance scams have also seen a surge in recent years, preying on victims' trust and emotions. In 2022, nearly 70,000 people reported being victimized by such schemes, resulting in a total loss of $1.3 billion. These scams often involve perpetrators creating fake relationships to manipulate victims into financial transactions.

Moreover, phishing attacks continue to be a dominant threat. The Anti-Phishing Working Group (APWG) noted that in the third quarter of 2022, 23.2% of all phishing attempts targeted the financial sector. During this period, email scams involving advanced fee fraud schemes increased by a staggering 1000%, demonstrating the evolving tactics used by cybercriminals.

These statistics are not just numbers; they represent real individuals whose lives have been disrupted by cybercrimes. The emotional and financial toll on victims is profound, often resulting in loss of savings, compromised personal information, and a deep sense of betrayal.

This book shares the firsthand accounts of those who have encountered these scams, providing insights into the methods used by cybercriminals and the impact on their victims. By understanding these stories, readers can better identify potential threats and develop strategies to protect themselves in the digital realm.

Through these narratives, it becomes clear that awareness and education are crucial in combating cyber threats. Empowering individuals with knowledge about the nature of these scams and the tactics used by perpetrators is the first step towards creating a more secure digital future.

While it is sad to read about what happened to Sarah and Marcus, it could happen to anyone. You might have even been a victim, or you came close —a suspicious email you ignored, a pop-up that made you pause.

This book has not been written to mock or shame anyone but to show everyone who reads it what lies beneath the surface of different moments and give you some tools to help you protect yourself even as these perpetrators of evil keep advancing their craft.

Through the harrowing experiences told as stories, we will take a dive into real stories, breaking down how the events happened in a general overview and why they are very effective even to the least suspicious individual. Along the way, you'll uncover practical lessons you can apply to your own digital life.

But don't think of this as a boring manual or a technical lecture. It's a journey into real-life scenarios, where ordinary people face extraordinary deception. You'll feel their tension, wrestle with their decisions, and see the world of cybercrime through their eyes.

In the chapters that follow, we will explore various types of scams, from phishing emails to romance frauds, exploring each one and providing practical advice on prevention and response. Through these stories, we aim to shed light to the often-hidden dangers of the digital world and equip readers with the tools needed to protect themselves and their loved ones.

The digital age offers a wide variety of benefits, but it also requires vigilance. By staying informed and cautious, we can enjoy the advantages of technology while minimizing the risks posed by those who seek to exploit it.

What Awaits You

In the pages ahead, you'll encounter stories like Sarah's and Marcus's—some unsettlingly familiar, others surprisingly eye-opening. Each chapter will pull you deeper into the web of cybercrime, showing you how these traps are laid and how to spot them before it's too late.

Whether it's a text message offering a fake prize, a social media scammer pretending to be your friend, or a fraudulent investment promising riches, the threats are closer than you think. But so are the tools to defend yourself.

By the end of this book, you'll not only recognize the traps but also understand the psychological tricks that make them so effective. You'll know how to respond, how to stay vigilant, and how to protect yourself and your loved ones.

For now, though, you're at the starting line. You've seen Sarah's email and Marcus's click. What happened after they acted? The answers are waiting in the chapters to come.

Let's get started.

Chapter 1: The Hook

Going through the stretch of the day, Sarah's evening was chaos. Dinner plates clattered in the sink as her two kids argued over whose turn it was to walk the dog. Her work laptop sat open on the kitchen counter, glaring at her with a good number of unanswered emails, and the phone in her hand buzzed incessantly with notifications. She exhaled sharply, pinching the bridge of her nose.

Then her eyes caught it.

The subject line in her email inbox that got her attention, it read *"Unauthorized Access Alert: Action Required."*

Her heart raced fast. It was from her bank—the logo was unmistakable, the tone urgent. It read "Dear Valued Customer, we have detected suspicious activity on your account. To secure your funds, please verify your details immediately by clicking the link below."

Her body jerked.

"Mom, he's not listening to me!" her daughter grumbled in the background, but Sarah barely heard her. Her eyes darted back to the email. The thought of someone emptying her savings gripped her chest like an anchor. The message looked neat, professional - just like all the other bank communications she'd received. The link at the bottom was blue, crisp, and inviting. *"Click here to verify your account,"* it urged.

But something tugged at her subconscious. Was this... off? She couldn't put her finger on it, but the timing was strange. She hadn't used her debit card all day. How could there be suspicious activity? It was now late in the evening, the Bank would have closed, she thought. Could she wait till morning?

Her mind spiraled.

What if the scammer already had access? What if every second she delayed meant losing more money?

Her hands trembled as she hovered over the link. Her kids were still yelling, the dog was barking, and her phone vibrated again on the counter. Everything was too loud, too much.

"I don't have time for this," she muttered under her breath. She clicked the link.

The Aftermath

The page loaded instantly. Looking very official, it had the bank's signature colors and its familiar logo. A form appeared, asking for her login details, her password, and her debit card PIN.

Sarah's urgency drowned out a faint sense of unease. After all, this was her bank. She couldn't risk leaving her account exposed. She filled in the fields and hit Submit!

When the page refreshed to "Error 404: Page Not Found," her stomach lurched. She stared at the screen, hoping it was some kind of glitch.

Not long after, her phone buzzed. A shocking text from her bank greeted her in reality - "$4,800 withdrawal request received. If this wasn't you, please call immediately."

Her hands shook violently as she dialed. The automated message droned on about high call volumes, and Sarah's frustration boiled over. By the time she reached a representative, her voice was sharp, her words spilling out in frantic bursts.

"I just got this text," she snapped. "Someone's stealing my money! I need you to stop it, right now!"

"Ma'am," the representative's voice was calm, infuriatingly so, "we'll do everything we can to assist, but I need you to answer a few security questions first."

Sarah screamed. Every second felt like a lifetime now. The questions blurred together; her date of birth, her mother's maiden name. When the representative finally confirmed her identity, Sarah's heart was pounding uncontrollably.

"We've frozen your account to prevent further unauthorized transactions," he said. "Unfortunately, the funds that have already been withdrawn cannot be recovered."

"What do you mean, they can't be recovered?" Her voice rose, trembling.

"Ma'am, this appears to be a phishing scam. Because the information was willingly provided, we cannot classify this as unauthorized access."

"Willingly provided?" Sarah nearly shouted. "I thought I was on my bank's website! You're telling me this is my fault?"

There was a long silence. The representative sighed. "I'm sorry, but yes, phishing scams rely on tricking users into giving away their personal information. Once the funds are transferred, they're often moved through multiple accounts to make recovery impossible."

Sarah's vision blurred with tears.

As the representative continued with cautioning words "Next time you receive a mail like this, you should either call the bank or log in to your online account to see if there are any pending updates and if your account looks accurate," Sarah was deep in thought, barely listening, bursting into a wail.

A Night of Reckoning

That night, Sarah sat on the edge of her bed, staring at the bank statement on her phone and prancing. $6,000 gone. Half her savings.

She couldn't stop crying. The numbers on the screen felt like a slap in the face, a cruel reminder of how easily her life had been upended.

Her kids, sensing her tension, approached cautiously. "Mom, are you okay?" her daughter asked.

Sarah snapped. "Just go to bed! Now!"

Realizing that the tone of her voice was very harsh than she had intended, the look on her daughter's face broke her heart. But she didn't apologize. She couldn't bring herself to it.

Her mind just kept replaying the moment she clicked the link, over and over. It was like a nightmare on repeat. Why hadn't she paused? Why hadn't she noticed the little things, the sender's email address, the awkward phrasing in the message? She felt stupid, reckless, and helpless.

Beyond the action, the weight of the consequences pressed down on her: the mortgage payment she couldn't make this month, the summer camp her kids might have to miss, the nagging realization that she'd let her guard down in a moment of chaos. No one was coming to rescue her.

The Real Cost of a Click

Phishing scams don't just take your hard-earned money--they strip you of your sense of security and stability, leaving you drowning in a sea of overwhelming guilt and self-doubt that creeps into every aspect of your life.

Sarah's story is painfully common, as this has been the experience of thousands of people. Scammers rely on fake authenticity, urgency and fear to override logic. They thrive in moments of distraction when you're overwhelmed and least likely to scrutinize an email or question a request.

For Sarah, the consequences were devastating. Her bank refused to cover the loss, citing her "willing participation." She spent weeks running around to sort out bills, maxing out all her credit cards, and explaining to her kids why they couldn't afford the things they had planned for. After the experience, the financial strain was only a fraction of the damage. The emotional toll that followed; the sleepless nights, the self-blame, the ridicule she condemned herself to; was harder to heal.

Lessons for the Rest of Us

Sarah learned the hard way, but her experience can teach the rest of us to be vigilant and proactive. Here are some key lessons that would have helped her and can help us also:

Verify Always, Don't Trust.

Even if an email looks legitimate, always verify through another channel. Go directly to your bank's website, your online banking account, or call them using a number you trust; not one provided in the email. Usually, the contact numbers are on the back of your cards or on the website.

Examine the Details.

Phishing emails often have subtle mistakes that the eyes can catch including odd sender addresses, misspellings, or generic greetings like "Dear Customer." These are red flags.

Slow Down.

Scammers create a sense of urgency to force you into acting without thinking. If something feels rushed and out of place, pause. A moment of hesitation can save you thousands of dollars. Trust your gut at these instances.

Educate Yourself.

Stay informed about common scams and share what you learn with friends and family. The more people know, the harder it is for scammers to succeed.

While Sarah's story is sore to the belly, it is a wake-up call for all of us. Phishing Scams are everywhere and take different forms exploiting human emotions from stating banking intrusions, to luring people on click baits that promise them that they have won prizes or vacations or vouchers and posing as legitimate sources. These scammers get clever and evolve but the signs are all the same regardless of the tactic they employ. With awareness and vigilance, you can protect yourself and your loved ones from becoming the next target.

Chapter 2: Trusted Voices

A cup of chamomile tea never hurt anyone after a stressful day Nadia thought to herself as her phone buzzed just as she was settling onto the couch, cup in hand. It had been a long day, and she was looking forward to a quiet evening of reading. The text on her screen stopped her mid-sip.

"Mom, I lost my phone. I just got this new number. Can you text me back?"

Her heart skipped. The message wasn't from her daughter's usual number, but the word **"Mom"** gripped her attention. Nadia's daughter, Anika, was away at college in another state. She'd told Nadia the week before that her phone had been acting like it was about to give up its functions.

Nadia's fingers moved quickly over the screen.

"Anika? Is this you? What happened?"

The reply came almost instantly:

"Yes, Mom, it's me. My phone broke, and I'm borrowing a friend's for now. I wanted to let you know."

Nadia's concern deepened.

"Are you okay? Where are you?" she texted back.

"I'm fine, but I'm stuck, and I need your help. My wallet got stolen, and I can't get back home. Can you send me some money? Just enough for an Uber and something to eat. I'll pay you back as soon as I get my cards replaced."

Nadia's heart broke at the thought of her daughter stranded and scared. Anika was one never to ask for help unless she absolutely needed it, so this made it feel genuine. "Of course. How much do you need?"

The Red Flags

The reply was quick again: "Just $50, Mom. Here's the number for the transfer: [link]. Please, I'm really scared."

Nadia paused. Something didn't feel right. She scrolled back up, rereading the messages. Anika was usually more composed, even in tough situations. And why hadn't she called instead of texting?

She typed, "Anika, can you FaceTime me? I want to make sure you're okay."

The response came after a long pause: "I can't right now. My friend's phone doesn't have a camera. Please just send the money, Mom. I really need you."

Nadia hesitated, her thumb hovering over the payment link. The urgency in the messages gnawed at her. It was so unlike Anika to be this panicked.

But what if it really was her? What if she ignored the message and Anika was left stranded?

The Click

Nadia tapped the link and followed the prompts to send $50. It was a small amount, and if it could help her daughter, it was worth it.

Minutes later, her phone rang. It was Anika's real number, almost like her instincts told her something was up with her mom, only that she was a minute too late.

"Hey, Mom! Just checking in. How's your evening?"

Nadia froze. Her breath caught in her throat. "Anika?"

"Yeah. Are you okay?"

Nadia's voice now trembling. "You… you just texted me for money a few minutes ago. You said your phone was broken."

"What? No, I didn't. My phone's fine. Mom, what's going on?"

Nadia's stomach clenched. Her hands were clammy as she explained the text exchange feeling betrayed. Anika listened in stunned silence before saying, "Mom, that wasn't me. I think you've been scammed. What information did you give out?"

The Fallout

Panicked, Nadia called her bank to report the fraudulent payment. The representative was understanding but firm: because she had authorized the transfer, there was little the bank could do to reverse it.

"That's not the worst part, Mrs. Singh," the representative said. "If the scammers had you enter your details during the transfer, they may now have access to your account. I strongly recommend changing your passwords immediately."

Nadia's chest tightened. Immediately, she opened her banking app and right there, approved transactions from the past hour were staring at her. There were several large withdrawals already made—amounts far beyond the $50 she had sent.

Her eyes betrayed her as the tears began to roll, a mix of anger, fear, and overwhelming guilt. How had she not seen the signs? She only wanted to help her daughter, but now she was left with an empty account and the sinking realization that she had fallen into a trap.

An Expensive Click

Nadia spent the following weeks in a haze of anxiety. The scammers had drained the sum of $3,000 from her savings account before she'd been able to lock it. That was all the savings she had right now. She berated herself for not calling Anika first, for not questioning the strange details in the messages. She was acting on her maternal instinct to take care of her daughter and ignored the caution around it.

The emotional toll was worse than the financial loss. Nadia felt violated, it was as if someone had allowed themselves into her private life and exploited her love for her daughter. She got irritated at the buzz of her phone as it sent a wave of dread through her. She double-checked every text, suspicious even of legitimate messages from friends.

Her conversations with Anika became strained, shadowed by Nadia's guilt and frustration. "Mom, it's not your fault," Anika had said more than once. But Nadia couldn't shake the feeling that she had let her guard down, and it had cost her, not just money but her mental and emotional health.

The Real Cost of a Text

Text scams like this, especially this family emergency kind, are cruel as they target the most vulnerable part of the victim, which is the love we have and the concern we show towards the people we care about. The scams are designed to bypass logic, quickly gathering information that can be used against us and tap directly into our emotions, making us act before we think.

Here's how they work:

- **Trust by Association:** The scammer starts out generically, or pretends to be someone you know, using a plausible story to gain your trust.
- **Urgency:** They create a sense of desperation, leaving you little time to question the situation.
- **Small Initial Request:** A seemingly harmless amount of money ($50, for example) lowers your defenses, but it's enough to give the scammer access to your account details.

Lessons for the Rest of Us

Nadia's story is a stark reminder of how quickly scammers can exploit our emotions. To protect yourself from falling victim to similar scams, here are some tips:

Verify Identity.

If you receive a message claiming to be from a loved one, call or video chat to confirm it's really them. Scammers often avoid calls because they can't mimic the voice or mannerisms of the person they're impersonating. Mostly, a video chat clears up all doubt. You can also install apps like True caller to verify numbers or use that of your cell phone provider if they have call filtering available.

Question Unusual Behavior.

Think about how the person usually communicates. Would they send a text like this? Would they avoid calling?

Be Wary of Payment Links.

Avoid clicking on links in unsolicited messages. Instead, use trusted methods to send money, especially if you have sent money to them before.

Act Fast if You Suspect a Scam.

Contact your bank immediately to freeze your account if you realize you've fallen victim. Reporting it quickly can limit the damage.

Don't Fall for the Variation.

Some other variation of this scam is unsolicited texts about unsuccessful parcel delivery or promos from your phone service provider or payment deposits. These variations are more terrible than the family emergency scam as they act fast to gain your information. Except you are expecting a parcel, some money or promo from your service provider, do not engage with the text, and if you are expecting any of these, verify with the senders or your providers respectively.

Nadia's story highlights the devastating effects of SMShing scams but also serves as a call to action. By staying vigilant and verifying before acting, you can save yourself emotional trauma by protecting yourself and your loved ones from the same fate. The next time you receive a message asking for help, pause. Ask questions. It could save you far more than money, it could save your peace of mind and emotional wellbeing.

Chapter 3: Sounds like Deceit

Stealing some time after her meeting to get some groceries, a voice call comes through her phone just as Maya was stepping out of the grocery store, juggling her totes full of groceries, keys, and a latte she had also picked up as a reward for surviving the last few hours. Barely seeing the number that flashed on her phone screen, though it was unrecognizable but local, her latte precariously balanced between her hands, she fumbled, and her thumb accidentally swiped "Accept."

An automated voice boomed through her ear pods in her ear, startling her so much she nearly dropped her coffee.

"The number associated with this service provider will be suspended. Listen to the following options to avoid suspension."

Maya froze mid-step, her world almost capsizing. Suspended? She asked herself, How? She couldn't have her phone cut off as everything she did ran through it. She gripped the phone tighter and pressed **1** to speak to a representative, as instructed by the robotic voice.

After a few beeps, a smooth, friendly voice answered.

"Hi there! Thank you for calling. My name is Jason, and I see you've been transferred to me because your account is at risk of being suspended. Don't worry—I'm here to help."

Jason's tone was light, almost cheerful, with the kind of energy that gives the assurance that everything is under control. Maya relaxed a little. If only she knew that she was just a victim of vishing, a scam that uses voice messages to derail people to act under duress.

"Oh, thank goodness," she said, bursting into a nervous laugh. "I can't lose my phone. My boss would kill me."

Jason chuckled. "We don't want that to happen to you now, do we? Let me look through your account to see what the issue is". Maya responded in affirmation as Jason chatted away. "Hey, I checked your account, and it seems the last few payments bounced. Nothing major—I can fix it for you in just a minute."

"Really?" Maya asked, regaining her composure as she stepped into her car. "You're a lifesaver."

The Lure

Jason's voice was warm, with just enough charm to put Maya at ease. He began with an easy laugh.

"Don't worry, there's no major cause for alarm and no penalties as well. This is just a minor hiccup we see happening all the time, especially with the way these systems are set up. Honestly, it sometimes appears like they're looking for ways to confuse people."

Maya chuckled, her grip on her phone loosening a bit. "Yeah, tell me about it. I can barely keep track of all my subscriptions these days."

"Right?" Jason sighed dramatically.

He had won Maya on comfort as his tone made her smile. He didn't sound robotic or rehearsed, he sounded real, relatable.

"This is an easy fix. We just need to verify a couple of details to make sure the system updates your account correctly. Once this is done, I would have saved your job."

Maya sighed with relief. "Thank goodness. I really thought I was about to lose my number. My whole life is on this phone! I've had this number for more that seven years now."

"Oh, trust me, I know how you feel," Jason replied with mock seriousness. "I lost my phone one time, and it was like I forgot how to function as a human. I couldn't call anyone, I couldn't check social media, I think I even forgot my girlfriend's birthday that year. Let's not let that happen to you, okay?"

Maya laughed, feeling her tension dissipated. "Alright, what do you need from me?"

"A few things," Jason said, slipping into a professional tone but keeping the friendliness intact, he was about to land the scam. I see you are using a MasterCard on file. He was not exactly sure of this, but knowing that most people use MasterCard, he led on with that. "Can you confirm the sixteen digits of your card? Just so we're looking at the right account."

She gave him the digits without a second thought. It was such a small thing, and Jason had been so casual, so nonchalant, that it didn't feel like a big deal.

"Perfect," Jason responded with a smile in his voice. "You're already making this easy for me. I wish all my calls went this smoothly. Now, just to double-check, what's the expiration date on that card?"

Maya rattled it off.

"You're a pro," Jason said, adding a slight chuckle. "Can I hire you to do my job for me? Because I think you'd crush it."

Maya laughed again. "Don't tempt me. I could use the paycheck."

"Trust me, it's not as glamorous as it sounds," Jason replied, leaning back into the humor.

"One last thing, and you'll be all set. Can you confirm the three digits at the back of the card usually called the CVV number and the billing zip code associated with the card? That way we can make sure everything matches perfectly in the system."

As Maya gave him the zip code, Jason clicked his tongue playfully. "And just like that, you're officially my favorite customer today. You're all set, Maya! You can be rest assured that you would not be getting suspended anytime soon and you get to keep your job."

She exhaled with relief. "You're amazing. Thank you so much."

"Just doing my own job," Jason said with a grin she could hear. "Now go enjoy the rest of your day, okay? No more interruptions, I promise."

Jason's light humor, personable approach, and incremental requests kept Maya from suspecting anything was wrong. By the time the call ended, she felt grateful, even lucky; to have had such a helpful representative, she was almost going to call the service provider back to give him a beautiful review.

The Calm Before the Storm

The call ended with a cheery farewell . She started her engine feeling relieved. Jason had been so understanding, even joking about how service providers seem to thrive on causing mild heart attacks.

By the time Maya got home and unloaded her groceries, she'd already moved on to other things, the call a distant memory.

For the next few days, everything seemed normal. Her phone worked fine, her texts went through, and her calls connected without a hitch. If anything, she was grateful for Jason's quick intervention.

It wasn't until her phone buzzed again, but this time with a call from her bank's fraud department, and this time things started to unravel.

"Ms. Zhang, we've detected a suspicious transaction on your account," the voice on the other end began.

Maya's countenance became low. "What kind of transaction?"

"It appears to be a large withdrawal made to an international account. We wanted to confirm if you authorized this."

"No! I did no such thing!" she said, her voice rising.

The Damage

Her bank account had been drained. Thousands of dollars, money she was saving together for her next adventure, gone in a single transaction.

Panic set in as Maya tried to piece it together. How could this have happened? She hadn't clicked any strange links or shared her account info to the best of her knowledge. Then it hit her. The call. Jason. The payment verification. She realized she had not gotten an official transaction receipt from her phone service provider since the transaction occurred; it became clear to her.

Her heart raced as she explained the situation to the bank representative. The representative sighed.

"Ms. Zhang, it sounds like you were the victim of a vishing scam. The caller pretended to be from your phone service provider with the end goal of gaining access to your payment information."

"But they only asked for my card details! I didn't give them my bank account info," Maya protested.

"Unfortunately, with the information you provided; your card number, expiration date, and billing zip code; they had enough information to create fraudulent charges."

Maya was numb as she tried to sit down, it felt like the blood in her body had dried up. The "friendly" Jason had been a mere thief, and she'd handed him the keys to her finances without even realizing it.

Over the next week, Maya had to fight with her bank to see if she could recover something from the stolen money. Unfortunately, the funds were unrecoverable because the transactions had been authorized using her details. The stress was overwhelming. She felt betrayed, filled with regret and anger at herself for not seeing the signs.

The Real Cost of Trust

Vishing scams like this one thrive on trust and charm, combining urgency with a friendly demeanor to disarm victims to the point that they trust them enough to hand over their information. Maya's experience highlights how scammers exploit our emotions and reliance on technology to gain access to our personal and financial information.

Here's how this scam worked:

- **Automated Urgency:** The call started with a robotic voice to create a sense of alarm.
- **Calm Reassurance:** The scammer's friendly tone coupled with humor made Maya feel at ease, lowering her defenses.
- **Incremental Requests:** By asking for small, seemingly harmless details, the scammer avoided suspicion while gathering everything needed to access her accounts, looking legitimate in the process.

Lessons for the Rest of Us

Maya's story serves as a wake-up call to stay vigilant, even when a situation seems harmless. Here's how to protect yourself:

Don't Trust Caller ID.

Scammers can spoof numbers to make them appear legitimate. Always verify the caller's identity by hanging up and calling the official number of the organization. Spoof in this context means mimicking to the best possible format.

Question Unexpected Calls.

If you're contacted out of the blue about account issues, ask questions. A legitimate representative will never rush or pressure you. Call your service provider to confirm as well.

Never Share Sensitive Information Over the Phone.

Payment details, PINs, and verification codes should never be shared in unsolicited calls.

Monitor Your Accounts.

Regularly check your financial accounts for suspicious activity and report unauthorized transactions immediately.

Use Alerts.

Set up fraud alerts with your bank or credit card provider to be notified of unusual transactions as soon as they occur.

Maya's experience is proof of how easily trust can be manipulated. But it's also a reminder that vigilance and skepticism can be your greatest defenses. The next time an unexpected caller asks for your information, take a breath, think through, and remember that even the friendliest voices can have ulterior motives.

Chapter 4: False Friends

Carla never tagged herself as someone who shared too much online, to the best of her knowledge, she did the bare minimum that social media expected. Her Facebook posts were harmless, a mix of infrequent family updates, her favorite recipes which dominated her page, and occasional rants about daily annoyances posted with the hashtag #TodaysRant. Her profile was set to "Friends Only," or she thought, and wouldn't unjustly add friends, except there was a connection, which felt safe enough. She was all about her privacy with the right audience.

Last week, she'd posted a photo of her home office setup, captioned: "Finally organized my workspace! Now if only my printer would cooperate...#TodaysRant" A few days earlier, she'd shared a milestone for her daughter with a picture and caption that read "Can't believe Jane is turning 10 next week. Where does the time go?"

Her timeline was a scrapbook of her life, from recipes to vacations to home projects to the occasional shared article about budget hacks for single moms. It never occurred to Carla that this collection of casual posts painted a detailed picture of her world.

But someone was watching.

The Watcher

Chris didn't message Carla immediately. That wasn't how he operated. Instead, he scrolled through her Facebook timeline, carefully analyzing her posts. Carla wasn't someone who overshared in the traditional sense, but to someone like Chris, her public posts were a goldmine.

In the past month alone, Carla had shared:

> A photo of her daughter's 10th birthday cake with the caption: *"Jane's big day! Can't believe she's double digits now, wow!."*

> A rant about slow Wi-Fi at home: *"Why do I pay for 'ultra-fast internet' when Zoom still freezes on me in the age of speed? Anyone know how to fix this?"*

> A tagged photo from her local coffee shop, with the caption: *"My Monday morning fuel! Matcha is bae!"*

To most people, these posts seemed harmless. To Chris, they were puzzle pieces, each one giving him a clearer picture of who Carla was, what she cared about, and most importantly, what he could exploit.

The First Contact

Chris made his move on Carla's Wi-Fi rant. He commented casually:

"Wi-Fi issues are the worst. But have you tried rebooting your router and checking the signal strength? If you want, I can walk you through some quick fixes."

Carla hesitated for a moment before replying. She didn't know Chris personally, but they were both members of the large community group on Facebook where she had shared her post, so she too had some ease in allowing him to help her. He seemed friendly, and his tips felt genuine at the end.

"Thanks for the tips! I'll give it a shot."

Chris replied with a thumbs-up emoji. He didn't push further. That wasn't part of the plan, at least not yet.

The Investigation Deepens

Over the next few weeks, Chris carefully built the conversations. He started liking more of Carla's posts as they had now friended each other, he also left thoughtful comments that were very supportive but never overbearing.

When Carla posted about Jane's birthday, Chris interjected: "Happy Birthday to Jane! That cake looks amazing. Did you bake it yourself?"

Carla replied proudly, sharing that she had indeed baked it, even mentioning Jane's love for chocolate.

Later that week, Carla shared a post about her latest DIY project—a reorganized home office. Chris used the opportunity to ask, "Love this! What kind of monitor is that? I've been thinking of upgrading mine."

Carla responded without hesitation, giving out the brand and model, she was becoming more open with Chris.

Each interaction seemed harmless, but for Chris, he was collecting data.

The Long Game in Action

A few days later, Chris sent Carla a private message about her Wi-Fi issues.

"Hey, I just noticed another post that says your internet is acting up again. Looks like the internet demons are after you, do you need help troubleshooting it? I work in tech, so this stuff is second nature for me. Send me details of your router settings, let me look into it."

Carla hesitated, but the offer seemed very genuine. And why not? He'd been helpful and friendly so far.

She sent him a screenshot of her router settings, as he'd requested. Chris guided her through resetting it, even suggesting changes to improve the speed.

"There! That should do it. Let me know if it's still giving you trouble."

Carla thanked him, feeling grateful for his help.

What she didn't know was that the screenshot had revealed her network name, her router's default IP address, and the password she hadn't bothered to change since installation.

Chris now had access to her network and could monitor her online activity.

The Gradual Probing

Chris didn't stop there. Over time, his questions became subtly probing, though they never felt invasive. He would ask questions like: "Do you use budgeting apps? I've been trying to get better with saving."

Carla replied, mentioning the app she used and how it linked to her checking account for convenience.

"Have you ever thought about backing up your files online? I keep everything on Google Drive, it's such a lifesaver."

Carla agreed and even mentioned how she used the same platform for her photos and important documents.

Each response Carla gave seemed like small talk, but for Chris, it was ammunition. He was building a complete profile of her digital life, putting everything he needed to exploit her together, piece by piece. He had the time, and she was not the only one he had in his books should his plans go sideways.

Trust Through Familiarity

Chris was careful to reinforce the illusion of trust. He would often share relatable struggles, thus making Carla feel like they had a lot in common.

When she posted about balancing work and parenting, Chris commented: "Tell me about it. Between work deadlines and my kids' soccer games, I'm surprised I even have time to breathe." If only he really had a kid.

His humor and empathy disarmed her, making him seem more like a friend than a stranger.

He also shared insights and advice that were useful and practical, for instance, he recommended tools to organize her schedule or apps to track her personal and business expenses. Every interaction reinforced his role as a helpful, trustworthy figure in Carla's online world.

The Subtle Web

By the time Chris was ready to strike, he had everything he needed. These included information like:

- **Carla's kids names and birthdays:** Perfect answers for security questions and pins.
- **Router access:** Gained through screenshots she willingly sent and casual troubleshooting help.
- **Financial habits:** Including the budgeting app linked to her bank account. Also tracking codes included in referral links he sent to her for the tools he recommended to her.

- **Schedule and routines:** Based on her posts about work hours and the kids activities outside of school.

He had constructed a detailed profile of Carla's life, and he did it without raising a single alarm. She willingly gave out every bit of information.

The Strike

It was supposed to be time to grab a latte Friday morning when Carla first noticed something was wrong. She had received a series of email notifications on her phone that read:

"Password reset requested for your Google account."
"Password successfully changed for your budgeting app."
"New login detected from an unfamiliar device."

Feeling immediately overwhelmed, she tried to log in to her accounts, but her passwords no longer worked. She clicked the "Forgot Password" option, but the recovery emails she expected to receive never arrived.

While she was in the process of understanding what was happening, her phone rang, snapping her out of her current predicament.

"Ms. Lopez, this is Rebecca from your bank's fraud department," the caller began to speak. "We've noticed unusual activity on your account. Did you authorize a $9,500 wire transfer to an international account this morning?"

Carla's voice shook. "No! I didn't authorize anything like that!"

"Thank you for confirming. Unfortunately, it appears that someone has accessed your account. They've used the information linked to your profile to bypass our security measures," Rebecca said.

Carla clenched her phone tightly, her heart pounding double the rate it previously beat just before the call. "How did this happen? I don't understand—I never gave anyone my bank details."

Rebecca paused. "Have you given anyone access to your Banking information lately? Do you have information that people can easily put together to guess your passwords and other information that pertains to you? Have you shared any personal details online recently?"

Carla's mind swayed as she replayed the last few months of her interactions with Chris. The router screenshots. The casual questions about budgeting apps. The friendly banter about her daughter's birthday.

She realized, with piercing horror, that Chris was collecting information on her life like puzzle pieces—and she'd handed them over like a willing participant.

The Blow

Carla spent the rest of the day on the phone with her bank and various customer support lines, trying to salvage what she could from her finances. Most of the funds were gone, transferred into untraceable accounts that her bank could not recover. Thankfully, the Bank's fraud systems could trigger an unusual behavior alert that saved her from becoming penniless. If that alert did not kick in and a temporary block added to her account, she would have been left with a different story.

She had now been locked out of her Google account, it was unrecoverable, along with years of personal photos, tax documents, and financial records stored in her Drive. Every attempt to reset her access failed; the recovery email had been replaced, and the security questions with the likely answers derived from her Facebook posts had been changed now.

It was a disastrous financial loss, but more than the finances, the emotional toll cut deeper. Carla felt violated, as though someone had broken into her home and rifled through her most personal belongings with her full permission.

For weeks, she was plagued by guilt. How could she have been so blind? She replayed every conversation with Chris, every post she'd shared, searching for the moment she should have realized something was off.

Her trust in social media and her trust in people was shattered. She immediately deleted her Facebook account after investigating Chris and finding out that he no longer existed on Facebook. She was too afraid to risk another scam.

The Real Cost of Sharing

Carla's story is not just about financial loss. It's about the cost of misplaced trust that has been placed in the digital age. Social media fraud like these preys on our tendency to overshare, even when we think we're being careful.

Chris's long game relied on Carla's casual approach to her online presence. By cleverly piecing together small details including her daughter's name, her use of Google Drive, her budgeting habits, he built a complete profile of her life and exploited it to devastating effect.

This intelligent scam didn't involve a single careless click or a moment of distraction. It was slow and calculated, a manipulation of trust leading to willful surrender unknown to Carla. This proves that even the most seemingly innocent interactions can have dangerous consequences.

Lessons for the Rest of Us

Carla's experience serves as a powerful reminder to rethink how we interact online. Here are key takeaways to protect yourself from similar scams:

Be Mindful of What You Share.

Even seemingly harmless details, like family names, birthdays, favorite colors or pet names, can be used against you. Regularly audit your social media posts and remove anything that could answer common security questions easily.

Verify New Connections.

If someone reaches out online, especially in a helpful or friendly way, take the time to verify their identity. Ensure you engage your privacy settings in adding new connections. Also, look for inconsistencies in new friend's profiles, and don't be afraid to ask mutual friends if they know the person or if the profile is authentic in a case where you sense foul play.

Limit Personal Information.

Avoid sharing technical screenshots, financial habits, or travel plans. These can provide scammers with crucial details to tailor their attacks, especially with sophisticated tools thanks to artificial intelligence.

Enable Two-Factor Authentication (2FA).

Use 2FA for all your accounts, especially those containing sensitive information. This adds an extra layer of security, even if someone gains access to your passwords. As long as you have another authentication process in place it becomes difficult for your account to be compromised.

Pause Before Engaging.

If someone you don't know offers help, take a moment to consider their motivations. Scammers often use friendliness as a tool to lower your defenses and once they earn your trust, there's no stopping what information they can get from you.

Monitor Your Accounts Regularly.

Set up account alerts to notify you of suspicious activity immediately and review your financial statements often. Change your passwords regularly especially when you have been notified of a breach on a particular account.

Carla's experience brings a sober reminder that not everyone online is who they identify themselves to be. In the digital world, trust is a currency, and scammers are experts at exploiting it.

The next time someone you hardly know offers unsolicited help or takes an unusual interest in your life, pause and ask yourself *"What do they stand to gain?"* Your caution might be the only thing standing between you and the next Chris Andrews.

Chapter 5: Piecing It Together

The perks of working from home meant that Marcus did not have to wake up bright and early. He had a late night catching up on one of his favorite shows and woke up just in time to prepare for his first meeting. To start his day, he would usually scan through his physical mail and then check his electronic mail. This was the beginning of a new month and as such, he should have received his bank statement for the previous month.

The bank statement arrived as usual, tucked between junk mail and a few bills. Marcus didn't notice anything unusual at first. But as he skimmed through the transactions, something caught his eye. It was a $3,600 charge from an electronics store in Mexico City.

Upon seeing it, he laughed loud saying to himself that he wished he was in Mexico at the moment but coming to reality, his brow tightened. He had not made a trip outside the U.S. in years, let alone bought anything in Mexico. Immediately, he picked up his phone and called his bank.

"I noticed a transaction on my account that I would like to dispute, I didn't make this purchase," he said firmly. "This must be a mistake." He paused.

The representative, with a friendly tone, listened patiently, then asked to put him on hold to investigate. When they returned, their tone was cautious.

"Mr. Price, we can definitely dispute the charge, but it looks like there are other unusual activity on your account based on what you have said. Have you recently applied for any new credit cards with us?"

Marcus froze. "No... Why?"

The representative sighed. "I can see that there's a credit card to the tune of $10,000 in your name that was issued last month, and several large transactions have been made on it."

"I didn't do any of that! Someone must have mistakenly done that on my behalf. Can you tell me how the application was made? I never received a card"

"It seems likely that someone used your information to apply for this credit card, sir," the representative said. "You may want to check your credit report and file a fraud alert immediately. I will go ahead and add a fraud watch on the account for you as you may be the victim of fraud."

The Unraveling

Marcus, feeling unsettled, ran to his car and sat there, staring at the credit card statement and replying to the conversation with the agent in his head. After spending an hour convincing this customer service representative that the $3,600 electronics purchase in Mexico City wasn't his, the call ends with unsettling news that his account had another credit card he didn't recognize and worse, that card had been overdrawn.

His thoughts raced. He couldn't imagine how this had happened. His finances were in order, his accounts were secure, or so he thought.

Unable to shake the nagging worry, Marcus logged into a credit monitoring site. The moment the report page was loaded, his chest tightened.

"Delinquent accounts: 4."

He scrolled through the list, his disbelief growing with each entry on the list.

A luxury car loan in Germany, unpaid for six months.

Another credit card with $12,000 in charges that was issued in Canada.

A payday loan of $7,500 in Singapore that was already in collections.

A pre-approved mortgage application in the United Kingdom.

A long list of accounts lay in the trail. The names, amounts, and locations blurred together. Marcus's hands shook as he clicked on the details, each more baffling than the last. He hadn't been to any of these places, hadn't opened any of these accounts—but the evidence said otherwise. Had had become a victim of not just fraud but identity theft.

The Global Damage

The next morning, Marcus received a call from a collections agency. "Mr. Price," the man began, his tone quite unfriendly, "we're calling to discuss your overdue loan payment. The balance is $7,500, and the lender has flagged it as delinquent and transferred it to us to collect on their behalf."

Marcus's voice faltered. "What loan? I didn't take out a loan."

"This is regarding the payday loan issued in Singapore last month, the man retorted. Are you saying you didn't authorize it?"

Marcus hung up before the agent could respond. His heart was pounding. Payday loans? Mortgages? Cars? It didn't make sense.

Over the next week, calls kept pouring in. He got an email from a law firm in Germany that informed him of a pending legal action for failing to make payments on a leased luxury car. To make matters worse, a government agency in Canada flagged his name in connection with a tax evasion case tied to a fraudulent business registered in Toronto under his Social Security number.

Each discovery was a literal blow to the chest. Marcus immediately felt like a stranger in his own life, his name now tied to crimes and debts spanning the globe.

The Human Cost

At just 37, Marcus was already building a promising life. His career as a project manager had taken off, and he was living as prudently as he could try as he was saving for a down payment on his first home. But with the chaos that followed the identity theft, he was left in despair.

The collection calls and fraud alerts became the order of the days that followed. His nights were worse as he lay awake, his mind replaying every discovery, every accusation, every denial and the possible source to the identity theft. He started looking physically stressed over a few nights with headaches that wouldn't go away, weight that he couldn't seem to keep on, and a hollow ache in his chest that made him feel like he was unraveling from the inside.

Everything concerning him suffered. Invitations from friends and colleagues went unanswered as Marcus withdrew from his social circle feeling very embarrassed and overwhelmed to explain what he was going through. His sister, Amanda, was with him to provide support and called often to check in, but even those conversations grew strained.

"You're shutting everyone out," she said to him one evening. "We just want to help."

"You don't get it, Amanda," he snapped. "This isn't something you can fix."

The guilt hit him immediately, but he couldn't bring himself to apologize.

Marcus began avoiding his family altogether, too ashamed of the mess that his life had become. He felt like a failure, someone who had let a faceless scammer dismantle everything he had worked for.

How It Happened

Marcus decided to search for answers and consulted a cybersecurity expert who specialized in identity theft and fraud. The consultant's findings were eye-opening and devastating.

The trail of his stolen identity began months earlier, pieced together through multiple sources:

- **A Job Hunt Gone Wrong:**
  While searching for work after a layoff, Marcus had uploaded his resume to several online job boards. One "employment agency" that reached out for a placement requested his Social Security number as part of the application process. Thinking it was standard procedure, Marcus provided it. There were indications that the website might have been fraudulent, including the bogus interview process but Marcus in his desperation had ignored that. The agency turned out to be a front for data thieves who sold his information on the dark web.

- **A Data Breach at a Retailer:**
  Marcus had made an online purchase at a major retailer that suffered a data breach. His name, address, and credit card details were leaked in the hack, giving scammers additional pieces of his puzzle. He did nothing to secure himself after that data breach.

- **Oversharing on Social Media:**
  On one social media platform, Marcus listed his full name, job title, and

employer, along with posts celebrating work milestones. On another social media platform, he had once posted a photo of a charity check with his address visible in the background. These details, combined with the stolen Social Security number, gave scammers a complete profile to exploit.

- **Phishing Emails:**

   The consultant showed Marcus a phishing email he'd likely clicked months earlier, disguised as an alert from his bank. It hadn't stolen money directly, but it had captured his login credentials, which were later used to bypass his account security.

"It's like putting together a puzzle," the consultant explained. "Each piece of information seems harmless on its own, but together, they give scammers everything they need to impersonate you."

The Ongoing Battle

By the time the dust started to settle, it was nearly a year, and Marcus was able to regain control of his identity. He had to file multiple fraud alerts with different credit bureaus in the different countries his information was used, had to dispute unauthorized transactions, and froze his credit to prevent new accounts from being opened.

Clearing his name wasn't straightforward. For instance, he had to prove he wasn't the one who rented the apartment in Brazil or applied for the loan in Singapore. Each claim required mountains of paperwork, hours of calls, and constant follow-ups.

Rebuilding his reputation was equally grueling.

His credit score remained low for multiple months, making it impossible to get approved for any type of loan or a new apartment. Employers hesitated when his background checks flagged fraudulent activity.

"It's like trying to put out a wildfire with a squirt gun," Marcus told Amanda during one of their attempts to reconcile. "Every time I fix one thing, two more pop up." Amanda was glad to have her brother back as she knew the issue was only temporary and that lessons had been learned.

Eventually, Marcus began taking proactive steps to protect himself:

- *He subscribed to an identity theft monitoring service that alerted him to suspicious activity.*
- *He removed unnecessary personal information from social media and deleted old accounts he no longer used.*
- *He adopted strict security practices, including using strong, unique passwords and enabling two-factor authentication on all accounts.*

"I'll never be that careless again," Marcus said to himself. "But I shouldn't have had to learn this the hard way."

The Real Cost of Identity Theft

Marcus's story isn't just about financial loss, it is a cautionary tale of how easily unseen hands can dismantle lives without care and in a brief moment. Identity theft doesn't just steal money; it robs trust, time, and peace of mind, often leaving victims to grapple with shattered futures. Stolen identities are weaponized to commit fraud, evade taxes, and fund criminal enterprises across borders, with effects that ripple far beyond the individual victim, impacting financial institutions, governments, and countless innocent people. The next time you're asked for personal information: whether online, over the phone, or in person, pause and consider the potential consequences if it falls into the wrong hands. Protecting yourself isn't just wise, it's essential.

Lessons for the Rest of Us

Marcus's experience serves as a wake-up call for everyone. Here's how to protect yourself from identity theft:

Monitor Your Digital Footprint.

Look over your social media profiles regularly and remove any unnecessary personal information. Google yourself from time to time and ask websites that carry your information without your consent to delete it.

Limit Publicly Shared Information.

Avoid posting photos or documents that reveal sensitive details, like addresses, car plates, bank logos, or account numbers. Any photo that might be able to reveal information about you should be kept away from the public eye.

Use Strong, Unique Passwords.

Protect your accounts with complex passwords. As much as possible, avoid using passwords that can be easily guessed. Enable two-factor authentication whenever possible.

Stay Alert to Data Breaches.

Monitor news about breaches affecting companies you use and take immediate action, such as changing passwords and enabling fraud alerts.

Freeze Your Credit.

Consider freezing your credit to prevent unauthorized accounts from being opened in your name. This is especially if you believe that you might have been compromised.

Invest in Identity Protection.
Use identity theft protection services to monitor your accounts and alert you to suspicious activity.

Marcus's story is a sobering reminder of how easily identities can be stolen and how far-reaching the consequences can be. The next time you share something online, pause. Ask yourself *"What could someone do with this information?"* Your caution today could save you years of heartache tomorrow.

Chapter 6: A Costly Love Illusion

Margaret quietly sat at her kitchen table, scrolling through Instagram while sipping on a cup of tea. At 62, she wasn't as tech-savvy as her grandkids, but she enjoyed staying connected with the world through photos and posts from friends. Instagram also helped her catch up on trends so she could express herself with her grand kids whenever they came around. Her feed was mostly filled with travel inspiration, recipes, and updates from her book club group.

One evening, as she admired a picturesque photo of the Amalfi Coast, a notification popped up:

"John Bradley has sent you a message."

While she didn't recognize the name, his profile photo showed a friendly-looking man with salt-and-pepper hair standing by a sailboat. Reading his bio, he described himself as a widowed engineer with a passion for travel, wine, and family, a combination that felt refreshingly normal compared to the flashy profiles she'd seen before.

Margaret hesitated for a moment before opening the message.

"Hi Margaret, I stumbled upon your profile through a travel page that we both follow. Usually, I don't do this, but I couldn't resist messaging you. Your posts give out such wonderful energy. Have you ever been to Italy? It's been on my bucket list forever!"

Margaret smiled unwittingly. It was a harmless and nice message. Without hesitation, she replied politely, sharing a bit about her favorite trips and joking about her dream of visiting Italy one day.

A conversation ensued.

The Long Game

Over the next few weeks, John and Margaret texted regularly. Their conversations were light and pleasant at first: exchanging travel tips, sharing photos, and bonding over their mutual love of wine.

Slowly, the messages grew more personal.

"You're a beautiful soul," he wrote to her one evening. "I can also tell that you have lived a life full of love and many adventures. It's rare to meet someone so genuine these days."

This made her smile.

For someone who had not had a companion in a while and as someone who was getting attention and the right compliments from this man, Margaret found herself looking forward to their chats. As a widow, she hadn't considered dating again, but John's warmth and attentiveness made her feel seen in a way she hadn't in years.

John opened up about his own story, a wife lost to cancer, an adult son working overseas, and a "career in civil engineering" that kept him traveling often. He sent photos of his work sites, his dog Pickles, and even a snapshot of a vintage bottle of wine he'd picked out on one of his trips, saying he hoped they could share it someday.

Margaret began to feel a spark, but she kept it to herself, not disclosing it to anyone. She told herself it was just friendship, a chance to have conversations with someone who understood her interests. But when John mentioned that he would be visiting her city soon for work, she couldn't deny the flutter of excitement in her chest. She brimmed with so much happiness.

The Twist

A week before his planned visit, John called Margaret. This was the first time they would speak over a call. His voice was deep and reassuring, with a slight British lilt she had not expected. They talked for long hours, sharing stories about their families, adventures and their dreams for the future.

Just as the conversation was wrapping up, John's tone shifted.

"I hate to do this," he began hesitantly. "But I'm in a bit of a jam."

Margaret's heart sank. "What's wrong?"

John explained that his latest project in Dubai had hit a snag.

His team was waiting on a shipment of materials that was critical to their work, but due to a banking error, the payment hadn't gone through.

"I've put all my time and money into this project," he said. "If I don't get it sorted by the end of the week, the project will collapse. I'll lose my investment."

Margaret felt a pang of sympathy. "That sounds terrible. How can I help?"

John, acting hesitant at first, spoke carefully after. "I'm so sorry I am asking, I would never do this if it weren't urgent, but if you could loan me $5,000 just until the funds clear, I'd pay you back immediately. You will be the hero in my books as you'll be saving my livelihood—and, honestly, my sanity."

Margaret was torn. The amount was significant, but John sounded so sincere, so desperate. She couldn't bear the thought of leaving him in such a dire situation. She thought to herself that they had become friends, and this was her opportunity to prove the worth of their friendship.

The Slow Drain

What Margaret did not know was that that first transfer was just the beginning of the real game. A week later, John called again, his voice heavy with frustration.

"Did you get my message with the screenshot of the statement? The payment still hasn't gone through," he said. "The bank claims there's an issue with the international transaction limits. I'm so embarrassed to ask, Margaret, but could you help me one last time?"

Margaret hesitated but agreed.

The pattern repeated itself over the next month. He would spend time with her flattering her with his well crafted words as he prepared her for his next exploit then give her a call when he had gotten her in the spot he wanted. Each time, He had a new excuse. These ranged from delayed payments to a legal fee, to a customs issue. Margaret would send the money reluctantly while assuring herself that John's situation would soon be resolved. She saw it as part of the risks of participating in international business.

On one occasion while catching up with her son, she mentioned the transactions to him, he grew alarmed. "Mom, this sounds like a scam," he said bluntly. "Have you even met this guy in person?"

Margaret felt defensive, insisting that John was real. He'd sent photos, called her, shared so much of his life with her. There was no way he could be lying.

Yet after that conversation with her son, a nagging doubt crept in.

The Devastating Truth

Margaret decided to confront John directly for more proof. When she called, the number went straight to voicemail. She tried again the next day, and the day after that, but she kept getting bounced to his voicemail. His Instagram account disappeared, and his emails bounced back as undeliverable.

Panicked, she decided to review their conversations, hoping to catch something that could lead her to him. The details she had initially brushed aside now felt glaringly suspicious: the generic photos, the polished tone of his messages, the oddly specific crises that always seemed to require just a bit more money, she felt stupid.

She reported the incidents to the authorities, who confirmed her worst fear after their investigations. "John Bradley doesn't exist," the investigator told her "None of the projects he requested assistance for exist as well". "This was a professional scam operation. They target older individuals on social media platforms, build trust over weeks or months before asking for money."

Margaret felt a wave of shame and grief. She had lost over $70,000 which was meant to be some of her retirement savings. Importantly, she had been left emotionally wrecked by a man she had fallen for who had never been real. Her heart ached for months; she was betrayed by love.

The Real Cost of a Scam

Margaret's story, while quite popular and works in different formats, is a harsh reminder of the devastating effects of love scams. These cons don't just steal victims money, they exploit trust, leaving victims to grapple with betrayal, guilt, and the loss of self-confidence.

Scammers often target older or vulnerable individuals, using social media platforms to appear credible and respectable. They rely on long-term manipulation, building emotional connections to disarm suspicion before striking. When they strike, they do it in bits to avoid suspicion till they believe they have milked the victim dry.

Lessons for the Rest of Us

Margaret's experience offers crucial lessons for identifying and avoiding love scams:

Be Wary of Unsolicited Messages.

If someone reaches out unexpectedly, especially on professional or social platforms, verify their identity before engaging. If you are absolutely unsure of who they are, it is best not to engage and delete the messages altogether.

Look for Red Flags.

Scammers often avoid video calls, make excuses for delays, and create elaborate stories to justify financial requests. If you sense a red flag, let your intuition be your best guide.

Never Send Money to Someone You Haven't Met.

Legitimate relationships don't involve sudden financial crises or urgent demands. If you have to send money, send what you can part with and if they harass you over it, know that it most likely is a scam.

Research Their Claims.

Reverse image searches on profile photos and checking public records can help expose fake identities. There are tools you can use to check if images are real or just stock photos

Involve Trusted Friends or Family.

Share your interactions with someone you trust, do not deal in silence. A second opinion can often catch red flags you might overlook.

Margaret's story is painful but vital. In the age of digital connections, vigilance is key. The next time someone you've never met asks for your trust or your money, pause and think. The cost of ignoring the warning signs can be far greater than you realize.

Chapter 7: A Race Against Time

No one would like to wake up to calls and messages from family, friends and colleagues about your private life being leaked on the internet, or would you? The day began like any other day for Danielle. Living the remote work life as a paralegal, her mornings were usually quiet. Her routine was simply a mug of coffee, her laptop open on the kitchen table, and the sound of her cat, Luna, padding around the house.

On this particular day, she was sifting through her emails when one subject line stopped her cold on her tracks.

"I've Been Watching You."

Danielle frowned. It looked like spam; the kind of nonsense email she usually deleted without hesitation. But something about this one felt… off. She hesitated then proceeded to click it open.

The message was short, but every word seemed to echo in her mind.

"I have been monitoring your accounts for some time now. I have all your account activities. I have enough information to bring you down, and I will publish it to the internet unless you pay me 10 Cryptos. If you delete this message, I will know. Do not report this to the authorities or format your computer, I will know if you do. My program is deep in your operating system, and you can't remove it. To get out of this, click the link below and initiate the payment. Once you're done, I will delete all the information I have and uninstall my program from your system."

She was in utter disbelief as her face painted horror. "This has to be a scam," she muttered to herself. But as she reread the email, some doubt began to creep in. What if it wasn't a scam?

The Growing Unease

In a snap, Danielle shut her laptop and pushed her chair back. She needed to clear her head, but the words from the email lingered. Words like "I have all your account activities."

She couldn't help but wonder, what did they mean by "activities"?

Were they bluffing, or did they actually have something?

As she searched within herself, her mind went to the most vulnerable corner of her life, her fiancé, Ethan. They had been in a long-distance relationship for two years, and as the relationship progressed, they shared intimate moments through photos and videos. Could they also have their call recordings? She thought to herself.

Danielle felt her face flush at the thought. There were many private moments that had been shared, meant only for the two of them. Could this person have intercepted them?

She tried to dismiss the idea. "No, that's ridiculous," she told herself. But the doubt just stayed stuck in her mind.

Unanswered Questions

The email's warning about deleting the message haunted her severely. Danielle opened her laptop again, carefully rereading the text to find any clues or foul play. She even Googled parts of it, hoping to find some reassurance that it was just a common scam.

Instead, she found forums filled with stories from people who had received similar emails.

"They threatened to leak my photos, but I ignored it, and nothing happened."

"Don't click the link—it's how they get you!"

Most of the advice was clear, don't engage the message. But some stories hinted at real consequences.

One post, in particular, caught her attention. "I thought it was fake until they sent me a screenshot of my desktop. They really were in my system."

Reading this post, Danielle's stomach churned. She glanced at the little green light on her webcam. Was she being watched now?

She immediately slammed the laptop shut again, but the unease was not going to vanish easily.

The First Signs

By morning, Danielle had decided to ignore the email. She hadn't clicked the link, so she figured there was no need to be concerned.

But as she started work, like her laptop was in on the scam, strange things began happening.

The laptop froze twice while she was drafting an email to a client, something that had never happened since she got it.

Danielle couldn't focus on work. Her mind kept jumping to the email. If this was a scam, why did she feel so uneasy?

Her phone buzzed; it was a text from Ethan.

"Good morning, babe! Hope your day's going well. Can't wait to talk later, I miss you."

As she stared at the message, the fear in her chest twisted into guilt. If the scammer leaked their private photos and videos, how could she explain it to Ethan? How could she live with the humiliation? Would she end up putting him in jeopardy also?

What if they'd already accessed her data? What if it was only a matter of time?

Desperation clawed at her so badly, she felt lost. Against her better judgment, she went for it and clicked the link in the email.

The Click

Danielle clicked the link.

Instantly, a dark webpage loaded, the screen was dominated by a countdown timer:

"48:00:00."

The instructions below were simple:

> Buy Crypto.
>
> Transfer the equivalent of 10 Cryptos to the provided wallet address.
>
> Wait for confirmation.
>
> Your time is counting down already.

The page promised that after payment, all information would be deleted, and the program would "uninstall itself." But beneath the reassurance there was another warning:

"Failure to comply will result in the immediate release of your files to your employer, friends, family and the world wide web."

Danielle felt trapped. She didn't know the first thing about Crypto, not even the price of Crypto. As she searched for tutorials on how to buy it, the thought of her private life becoming public made her chest tighten.

But the worst was yet to come.

The Trap

The webpage was stark and menacing: a black background, white text, and the timer ticking down.

"Make the payment before the timer reaches zero. Failure to comply will result in the immediate release of your files."

Danielle scrolled down, looking for more details. But as she spent time on the page, she didn't notice that ransomware was being automatically downloaded in the background. This would lock all her files upon installation and this time she would be in trouble for real.

By the time she closed the browser, it was too late.

Her laptop froze briefly, then restarted. Once the screen came back on, a new message greeted her saying,

"Your files have been encrypted. Pay 20 Cryptos to restore access."

Danielle gasped. "Twenty? It was ten before!"

Every attempt to open a file was met with the same message. Her work documents, her photos, her personal files, everything was locked.

The reality of the scam hit her like a tidal wave, she'd fallen into the trap.

The Breaking Point

Seeing that her actions had now caused significant damage, Danielle had to contact a cybersecurity firm, her voice shaking as she explained the situation.

"I think they've been spying on me," she said. "They might have my private photos and videos. What if they leak them? I was scared for my reputation"

The expert's tone was calm but firm. "These types of emails are often bluffs," he explained. "The real attack starts when you click the link. The ransomware encrypting your files is the actual threat. The initial message is just the push to make you click"

"But what about the pictures? What if they're real?"

"It's unlikely," the expert reassured her. "Attackers rely on fear to make you act irrationally. They want you to panic and pay before you realize they might not have anything at all."

Danielle felt a flicker of hope. But when the expert explained the process to recover her files without paying the ransom, her hope dimmed, but she felt relieved. The only surefire way to regain control was to wipe her system—and most of her files would be lost forever.

The Long Recovery

Danielle spent the next few weeks rebuilding her life. The cybersecurity firm helped her isolate the infected computer, remove the ransomware, and restore her operating system.

While thankfully, some of her personal files were backed up on an external drive, a lot of the most recent ones including work reports, private photos, and financial spreadsheets were gone.

She implemented stricter security measures going forward:

- Enabled two-factor authentication (2FA) on all her accounts.
- Stopped using the same cloud storage for personal and work files ensuring they are backed up separately.
- Began using encrypted apps to share private messages with Ethan.

After the devastating episode, even with the ransomware removed, Danielle struggled to shake the paranoia. Every email felt like a potential threat, every unexpected notification caused her to shiver.

The Real Cost of Fear

Ransomware scams like this don't just lock victims out of their files, they are designed to prey on their deepest fears. The mere suggestion that personal, private moments could be exposed was enough to make Danielle question everything she thought she knew about her security.

Scammers exploit shame and desperation to push their victims into irrational actions, knowing that fear is a powerful motivator. By the time victims realize they've been duped, the real damage which includes lost data, financial loss, and emotional strain would have already been dealt.

Lessons for the Rest of Us

Danielle's story brings up critical lessons for avoiding ransomware attacks:

Recognize the Fear Tactics.
Scammers often bluff about monitoring your activities. If you receive a threatening email, remain calm and seek expert advice before acting. Do not give in to fear even if you know that you have data that could be compromising.

Be Wary of Links.
Never click on links in unsolicited emails, especially those with threatening or urgent language. Never click on links you don't need access to. These include links you find on websites that you suspect might be fishy.

Backup Regularly.
Keep copies of important files on external drives or secure cloud storage to minimize damage from ransomware attacks or any type of attacks.

Use Strong Security Practices.
Enable 2FA, update your passwords regularly, and install reputable antivirus software to block threats.

Report the Attack.
Contact a cybersecurity professional or local authority to document the incident and protect others from falling victim by sensitizing them.

Danielle's experience is a stark reminder of how fear can cloud judgment. The next time you receive a suspicious email, don't hesitate. Think. Remember that no scammer's threat is worth sacrificing your peace of mind or your files.

Chapter 8: Too Good to Be True

Adrian wasn't actively looking for the bag that day. He was just winding down from a long workweek, lying down on his couch, he was scrolling aimlessly through his favorite online marketplace. He had even promised himself that he'd spend the weekend "window shopping" only—no actual purchases.

But when the image of *that* caramel leather designer bag appeared on his screen, all bets were off. It was as if he lost composure for all of one minute. But who would blame him?

It wasn't just any bag. It was *the bag,* like the Ferrari of business style bags. This particular one he had stared at longingly through department store windows, saved in countless Pinterest boards, and longingly added to his online cart only to abandon it when the $5,200 price tag stared him down.

But here it was, staring back at him for a meagre $500. And this was not some knockoff or "inspired by" version, either, the photos screamed authenticity. That was how much he had studied the bag.

He had an energy-filled ecstatic breathe as he read the description, "Like new. Only used twice. Authentic."

Convincing himself that this was some prank or glitch, he refreshed the page. But with every refresh, the listing was still there. His excitement immediately morphed into a frantic urgency as he started scanning for his wallet. What if someone else snagged it before he could? Heaven forbids, he said to himself.

He did a quick scan on the seller's profile, "100% Positive Reviews! Fast Shipping! All items authentic or your money back." It looked clean, legit, even.

Adrian barely remembered entering his payment details. His satisfaction hit a crescendo when he saw the "Payment Successful" notification followed by the confirmation email that hit his inbox, he felt an electric thrill.

"Five to seven business days," the email promised.

He leaned back in his couch, imagining the compliments he would get at the office and his response to the guys "Oh, this? Just a little find online." His best-kept secret, or so he thought.

The Anticipation Game

The first few days of waiting were painstakingly long in his eyes. Four business days felt like four weeks. Adrian tracked every email notification and delivery to his building like a hawk. He was eagerly looking forward to the delivery.

Day five rolled around, and his impatience grew. "Shipping delays happen," he told himself, brushing it off as a delay with his local post. But when day seven came and went with no package in sight, his excitement dashed.

He sent a quick message to the seller: "Hi there! Just checking in about the caramel leather bag. Can you provide a tracking number or an update about the delivery?"

Two hours passed. Then five. Then an entire day.

No reply.

By day nine, Adrian's polite tone turned firmer. "Hello, I haven't received any updates about my order. Can you respond as soon as possible."

Still nothing.

Panic set in when he decided to check the seller's profile. The once-pristine account, with its glowing reviews and promises of authenticity, had vanished, almost as if he had previously seen a mirage. In its place was an error message.

"This user does not exist."

His heart sank.

The Big Reveal

Adrian probed in denial. There had to be a logical explanation for this. Maybe the seller's account was suspended for some minor infraction, or they accidentally deleted their profile. He definitely knew he had not been scammed. Right?

He combed through his emails, searching for any scrap of information. The order confirmation? A useless string of numbers. The payment receipt? It linked to a generic email address with no contact details.

In that moment of realization, he felt tense. He had fallen for it.

The bag wasn't coming, there was no bag.

Adrian called his bank, trying to see if he could dispute the transaction as he explained what had happened.

"I authorized the payment, but the seller disappeared," he said, as he fumbled to put accurate words together. "Can you reverse it?"

The representative sighed. "I'm sorry, sir, but since the transaction wasn't flagged as fraudulent at the time, there's little the bank can do. You might want to contact the marketplace directly to dispute your claim."

Adrian felt embarrassed, he scolded himself for being careless. He sent an email to the platform's support team, but their response only confirmed what he already suspected. "Unfortunately, we cannot recover funds in cases involving fraudulent sellers. We expect buyers to perform their due diligence before making commitments. You can read about it in the company's policies."

Reality Check

For days, Adrian rotated between anger, embarrassment, and disbelief. Replaying the moments that led to the purchase, he dissected every red flag he had ignored.

The price was absurdly low, too good to be true for such a merchandise.

The seller's profile had a vague history, with generic reviews that now felt suspiciously fake.

The payment had been requested through a third-party app, not the platform's built-in system.

He felt stupid.

The worst part wasn't even the lost $500. It was the humiliation of knowing he had been duped. Adrian found himself in self doubt, he was too ashamed to confront his friends without the bag that he had bragged that he copped.

He wished he could track down the culprit, but he knows how impossible this would be as he was not smart about the transaction. He had let the excitement of the cost get to him.

A Humbling Moment

That weekend, Adrian visited his sister, Jasmine, who was notorious for sniffing out incredible deals from unexpected stores and sites without getting burned. Jasmine listened to Adrian's story with a mix of amusement and exasperation. Teasing him, she said,

"You thought you were getting a designer bag for $500?" Jasmine teased. "Come on, Adrian, you're smarter than that."

"It looked legit!" Adrian protested, throwing his hands in the air. "The photos were perfect, the profile seemed real… I mean, how was I supposed to know?"

Jasmine raised an eyebrow. "Did you reverse image search the photos? Did you check their reviews? Did you even look at the payment method?"

Adrian groaned, slumping into the couch. "No. I got too excited and clicked 'buy' without thinking."

Jasmine laughed. "Well, congrats on your $500 lesson in online shopping."

Adrian couldn't help but laugh too.

The Real Cost of a Bargain

Adrian's story isn't unique as it happens in many ways. Online shopping scams prey on our excitement and sense of urgency and want, pushing us to act impulsively before we think things through. For Adrian, it wasn't just about losing money, it was about the sting of realizing he had ignored all the signs that looked obvious.

These scams are designed to exploit desire, manipulating buyers into believing they've found the deal of a lifetime. But as Adrian learned the hard way, if something seems too good to be true, it probably is.

Lessons for the Rest of Us

Adrian's experience offers valuable lessons for navigating the world of online shopping:

If It's Too Good to Be True, It Probably Is.

Ridiculous discounts on high-priced items are often a red flag. Especially if they are sold at unrecognized retailers.

Research the Seller.

Look for detailed reviews, transaction history, and a refund policy. Google the seller to see if you can find information on them. Beware of new accounts or profiles with vague feedback.

Avoid Third-Party Payments.

Always use the platform's secure payment system to protect yourself in case of fraud. Avoid direct transfers or payments through other payment platforms that are not related to the marketplace you are using. If you must do a transfer or pay cash, meet at a public venue where you can alert people to help for your safety.

Check the Photos.

Use reverse image search to verify whether the photos in the listing are original or stolen from elsewhere. You can find tools online.

Pause Before You Buy.

Take a moment to evaluate the deal. A little caution can save you a lot of hassle.

Review the platform's buying and refund policies to ensure they protect you in some way or they have disclaimers. Plus, do you really need the product?

For Adrian, he learned that all that glitter is not exactly gold, maybe it can be fake gold-plated. We don't have to learn the hard way and part with money that could have provided value elsewhere. Next time you find a deal that is too good to be true, take some time to do your research before you commit your money to the purchase.

Chapter 9: Promising the World

Without thinking twice, James had convinced himself that he was not a gambler, or at least he thought so. There was this idea of making easy money that sometimes made him curiously restless even though he would eventually brush it away.

He was not a risk taker, but he did not hate taking risks whenever he needed or when he could avoid them. His savings sat in his bank account, growing slower than drying paint, and while he had never admitted it out loud, he sometimes wondered to himself "*What if there was a faster way?*"

One lazy Sunday afternoon, as he scrolled through his social media feed, an ad popped up, it was a video with an influential face encouraging people to try a new investment.

"Turn $500 into $5,000 in two weeks with this proven forex trading system. Limited spots available!"

James scoffed. This was obviously a scam. Who fell for this stuff anyway? He scrolled past but paused. It felt like something lured him. Maybe it was the video embedded in the ad, showing this influential person clicking through charts to explain the investments while their balance climbed. It could have also been the glowing testimonials from people with smiling photos, thanking the system for helping them "escape the 9-to-5 grind."

James shook his head but clicked anyway. His curiosity got the best of him. The website looked clean and professionally done, something you would expect from the calibre of influence behind it. There was a video from another influential figure welcoming people to the investment scheme and telling them how they had made the best decision for their financial freedom along with graphs, profit projections, and even screenshots of real payouts, complete with timestamps and transaction IDs.

A live chat box popped up.

"Hi, I'm Alex! I've been using this system for six months, and it's changed my life. Let me know if you have questions!"

James hesitated, while being skeptical, he was intrigued about how organized the website was with detailed and understandable information.

He typed a quick message saying, "What's the catch?"

Alex gave an immediate reply "No catch. We're a team of professional forex traders pooling resources. We do the trading, you just sit back and watch your money grow! We are backed by some of the world's heavy hitters too, which gives you a guarantee for your money."

James smirked. It sounded ridiculous to believe. But that flicker of intrigue had grown into a spark. He wasn't making any commitments, he reasoned. Just exploring.

"How do I start?" he typed, feeling convinced.

The Hook

To do this right, James would "test" the system with $500. This was money he told himself he could afford to lose. Honestly, he didn't expect anything to come of it, but when he got a notification three days later, he nearly dropped his phone in disbelief.

"Your investment has appreciated to $750. Would you like to withdraw your profits or reinvest?"

At first, his instinct pushed him to call it quits and take the money, but he hesitated. To see if it was real, he clicked "withdraw" just to see what would happen. Not up to an hour later, he received a $750 deposit notification in his bank account.

With this transaction done, most of his skepticism dissipated.

James messaged Alex, who responded with the same friendly tone "Glad to see you're doing well James! Let me know if you're ready to reinvest your profits. The more you invest, the higher your returns."

James nodded to himself. It made sense. If $500 turned into $750, then $1,000 could double. Right?

He invested another $1,000.

Over the next two weeks, James became hooked. His account balance climbed with every passing day. His $1,000 turned into $1,500, then $2,200. Without hesitation, he started reinvesting everything, chasing higher and higher returns.

Greed Sets In

As his gambling side revealed itself more, James could not stop talking about the investment. He did not talk to his friends; he spoke to himself. Every time he checked his account, he felt elated. He went ahead to create a spreadsheet to project his potential earnings, grateful that he took advantage of the opportunity he almost passed on for a scam.

By the end of the month, his balance had ballooned to a plumpy $5,000. It felt surreal. For the first time, James began to picture a future where he wasn't stuck grinding away at his office job. He was about to escape the rat race.

As he tried to withdraw a portion of his balance though, the system gave him an error message.

"Withdrawals temporarily paused due to system maintenance. Please try again later."

James frowned but didn't panic. He messaged Alex immediately, who responded quickly, "Sorry about that! We're upgrading our payment system to handle the high volume of transactions. Everything will be back to normal in 48 hours."

Two days later, James tried again. Same error.

That's when the phone call came.

"Hi, James! This is Mia from the VIP investment team. Congratulations on your incredible returns! How do you feel?"

Mia's voice was warm and professional, the kind of tone that would curtail any hesitation and put you at ease.

"We noticed you've been doing exceptionally well with our platform during this short time," she continued. "We would like to offer you an exclusive opportunity to join our VIP trading tier. This tier is for long term investors who love to see their investment grow with real potential. With just a $20,000 investment, you could see guaranteed returns of up to $40,000 in under two weeks!"

James froze. $20,000 was nearly all of his savings. But the idea of doubling his money in two weeks was intoxicating.

"This offer is only available for a limited time," Mia added. "But based on your track record, we're confident you're ready for this level of trading. You only need to act fast."

James bit his lip. He asked if he could think about it, but Mia gently reminded him of the time-sensitive nature of the opportunity, especially with the limited slots being available on a first come first serve basis.

That night, James barely slept, he thought about all the things he could do with his doubled funds. The next morning, without blinking twice, he transferred the difference of his investment to make up the $20,000.

The Let Down

The first few days felt like déjà vu. James's account balance climbed rapidly, first it hit $28,000, then climbed to $34,000, then $40,000 and it was not even two weeks yet. He grew excited and even started planning how he'd spend his earnings. He thought of paying off debt, or upgrading his car, or maybe even putting a down payment on a condo - this could help him expand into real estate investment.

But when the two-week timer expired, James noticed something strange. His balance froze just a little above the $40,000 mark.

He tried to withdraw, but the system crashed at every attempt. Panicking, he messaged Alex, only to find the chat box grayed out. He tried calling the hotline, but the number was disconnected.

Finally, he checked the business's website.

"Error 404: Page Not Found."

The realization hit him like a gut punch. The entire operation was gone. His savings, his excitement, his dreams—all vanished in an instant.

The Aftermath

In just two weeks, all his savings were gone. James spent weeks trying to recover his money. He filed reports with his bank, contacted the authorities, and even searched online forums for other victims. But the scammers outwitted him by covering their tracks perfectly.

He started realizing the obvious. The influencers who he had come across in videos were not backing up the platform in anyway, their presence was part of the con, the videos of them speaking were AI generated.

Furthermore, the initial payouts, James realized, were a trap. They had hooked him with small wins to build trust, only to wipe him out once they had ascertained that they had hooked him.

Worse than the financial loss was the shame. James couldn't bring himself to tell his friends what he had done. Every time he thought about the $20,000, his chest clenched. Just when he thought he wasn't a gambler, he gambled away his savings.

"How could I be so stupid?" he muttered to himself.

The Real Cost of Greed

James's story is a sober reminder of how easily greed and the fear of missing out (FOMO) can cloud judgment. Scammers know exactly how to play the confidence game to exploit our desires for financial freedom, using small successes to build trust and lure victims deeper into their trap.

For James, the pain wasn't just about the money. It was the betrayal of his instincts, the embarrassment he brought on himself, and the realization that he had ignored all the warning signs, especially that of getting his money doubled quickly.

Lessons for the Rest of Us

Here's how to protect yourself from falling into similar traps:

Beware of Small Wins.

Scammers often use small payouts to gain trust before asking for larger investments. If the payout is small but proportionate to the invested amount, beware.

Question High Returns.

Promises of guaranteed profits or unusually high returns are a major red flag. Research the underlying business that gives high returns if possible.

Research the Platform.

Look for independent reviews and verify whether the platform is registered with financial authorities. Don't fall for scams where they use important people to promote platforms as this is all a scheme using AI technology to mimic these people.

Avoid Pressure Tactics.

Urgent deadlines and "exclusive" opportunities are designed to rush you into making decisions.

Seek Professional Advice.

Before making significant investments, consult a trusted financial advisor even if you have done your due diligence.

James realized that these scammers confidently played on his emotions and his desire to make more money fast. He would have stopped at first try but greed crept in. It is the same for us, we see deals that are too good to be true and get pressured into investing in them, so we don't miss out. When you spot a deal that looks too good to be true, even if you feel like going all in, put your greed in check and only invest the amount of money you know you can afford to lose. Ask yourself, "Is this investment worth me losing my hard-earned money?"

Chapter 10: Help You Didn't Ask For

This particular Tuesday afternoon, just as he had settled into his favorite recliner with a mug of coffee and his tablet, Victor got the call that would change everything for him.

At 63, he prided himself on being self-reliant, getting by on his own with little or no help. As a retired accountant, he wasn't exactly tech-savvy, but he got by. He knew how to check his emails, stream his favorite detective shows, and play a mean game of online Sudoku. If something went wrong with his devices, he usually Googled his way out of it, or called his niece, Mia, the family's resident tech whiz to figure it out.

But today, as the phone rang, he knew deep down in his gut that something was off.

The number looked official, a local area code, no odd digits. With a small frown, he answered.

"Hello?"

"Good afternoon, sir," a calm, confident voice replied. "This is Ron, support personnel from Microsoft. I'm calling because our system flagged unusual activity on your computer. We believe it may be infected with a serious virus."

Victor sat up straight on his recliner. "A virus?"

"Yes, sir," Ron continued smoothly. "We've detected malware that's been sending out unauthorized emails from your account and slowing down the speed of your system. It looks like your system has been compromised, and your personal information may already be at risk."

Victor's pulse elevated. Malware? Unauthorized emails? System slowdown? He hadn't noticed anything strange, but what if he had missed it?

"I... I don't understand," he stammered. "How did this happen?"

Ron's tone was patient, almost fatherly. "It is hard to say, sir. Malware can come from anywhere, an infected website, an unsolicited click from a phishing email, even a routine download. But the good news is, our systems caught it early. If you have a moment, I can guide you through the steps to secure your computer."

Victor hesitated. "Are you sure you are from Microsoft? I can wait for my niece to come around and help me with this"

Ron chuckled softly. "I completely understand your concern, sir. You can verify our number on Microsoft's website, but I assure you, I'm here to help. If we don't address this issue quickly, it could escalate with the rate at which the virus is spreading. Identity theft, banking fraud..." His went off ominously.

The thought of losing control of his accounts already made Victor cringe. He had read about people having their savings wiped out overnight. He couldn't afford to take that risk.

"So, what do you need me to do?" he asked, gripping the phone tightly.

The Rattle

Ron's tone was steady and authoritative, the kind of voice that makes you feel like you were in capable hands.

"All right, sir, let's get started. Are you in front of your computer?"

Victor adjusted his glasses and sat down. "Yes, I'm ready."

"Good. First, I'll need you to open the command prompt."

Victor blinked. "The command what?"

"It's a small window where we can input commands," Ron explained patiently. "It's simple, just press the Windows key on your keyboard and the letter 'R.'"

Victor fumbled for the keys, following Ron's instructions. A small window appeared on his screen.

"Now type 'cmd' and hit Enter," Ron said. "A black box with white text should pop up."

Victor stared at the screen, his confidence already starting to waver. "I've never seen this before. What is it?"

"It's where we can run important commands to see what's happening on your system," Ron replied smoothly. "You don't have to worry, it's perfectly safe."

Ron began dishing out a series of instructions, asking Victor to type commands filled with slashes, letters, and numbers. The screen populated with lines of text Victor couldn't make sense of.

He looked rattled.
I can't make sense of any of this, he said.

Spotting the moment as this was the plan all along, Ron decided to capitalize on Victor's ignorance. His tone suddenly sounded concerned.

"This isn't good."

Victor's heart raced now sounding panicked. "What!?"

"It looks like your system is under active attack. This is serious, sir."

Victor felt his palms grow sweaty. "What do I do?"

Ron sighed, as though he hated to be the bearer of bad news. "The commands I've given you confirm the infection if you can't understand what you see, but this is beyond a simple fix. The good news is that I can help. I just need access to your system to run the advanced tools we have at Microsoft."

Victor hesitated, feeling more uneasy. "How does that work?"

Ron's voice softened, with a reassuring tone. "I'll guide you through the process. It's just like a technician visiting your home to fix a problem, the only difference is that I'll do it remotely. This is the safest and quickest way to ensure we stop the breach before any real damage is done."

Victor still wasn't sure. "Are you sure this is safe? I can get my niece to look at it when she is back from school"

Ron chuckled lightly, the sound disarming. "Sir, I understand your concern, but this is standard protocol. Think of it like calling a plumber to fix a broken pipe. You're still in control as I can only access what you allow. You will also be here all through and can see what I am doing. Shall we proceed?"

Victor took a deep breath. "All right. Let's do it."

Ron instructed him to open his browser and type in a specific web address. A small window popped up with the words "Allow Remote Access?"

Victor paused, his finger hovering over the mouse.

"This just gives me temporary access to your computer," Ron explained. "Once the issue is resolved, the connection will be severed. You're in safe hands."

Victor, still feeling hesitant, exhaled slowly and clicked "Allow," his screen came to life, the cursor moving on its own.

The Twist

Victor leaned back, uneasy.

"Is that you?" he asked.

"Yes, sir," Ron replied cheerfully. "I'm just running some diagnostics."

Victor watched as Ron navigated through unfamiliar screens, pulling up rows of cryptic numbers and error messages or so he thought.

"Oh dear," Ron muttered. "This is worse than I thought. Look at this, sir."

Victor squinted at the screen.

Ron had opened something called a "System Log," where rows of red messages blinked like sirens.

"These are all malware activities," Ron explained gravely. "Each one represents an attempted breach of your system. It's a miracle your accounts haven't been completely compromised yet."

Of course, all this was a ploy to sell Victor on the malware before he landed the scam.

Victor's stomach churned. He didn't understand the jargon, but the red warnings looked serious.

"Can you fix it?" he asked anxiously.

Ron sighed. "I can do my best, sir. But the damage is extensive. Your basic antivirus isn't strong enough to handle this. You'll need to upgrade to our advanced protection plan." He finally caught his break.

Victor frowned. "How much is that going to cost?"

Ron didn't miss a beat. "Our standard plan is $299 for the year, and our premium plan, which I recommend for maximum security, is $499 for the year. It's a small price to pay for peace of mind."

Victor's hand trembled as he reached for his wallet. "I guess… I guess I'll take the premium plan." He said hesitatingly.

The Betrayal

Ron guided Victor through the payment process, reassuring him that he'd made the right decision.

"You're all set, sir," Ron said finally. "I'll spend the next hour fixing your computer. You can go about your day, I'll call you once it's resolved."

Victor let out a sigh of relief. "Thank you, Ron. I really appreciate it."

But the relief was short-lived, not even one deserving thanks to Ron.

The next morning, Victor logged into his bank account to check on a routine payment. Instead of his usual balance, he saw a string of transactions he didn't recognize. Thankfully he logged in early to stop the bleed before his other accounts were affected and totally drained. On the account that was accessed, the following transactions were made including:

- $900 to an electronics retailer.
- $1,500 transferred to an unknown account.
- $3,000 labeled "Online Purchase."

Frantically, he called his bank.

"I didn't authorize these!" he exclaimed.

The representative's tone was firm but sympathetic. "It looks like your account was accessed from a different location. Did you recently log in to a public computer?"

Victor was confused. "No, he replied, I have my own computer." But then he remembered he had given someone else unauthorized access to his computer and information about his credit card.

The line went quiet.

"I'm sorry, sir," the rep said finally. "It looks like you've been scammed. But we can block your account and cancel your cards to ensure the scammer does not gain access to your other accounts but the funds that were taken are irrecoverable."

The Devastation

Victor was mad at himself, he should have trusted his gut and waited for his niece. He felt betrayed by the scammer, by his own trust, and by his lack of knowledge.

His niece Mia, the family tech expert, came over that evening to help him secure his accounts and wipe his system clean.

"Uncle Victor, you should've called me," she said gently. "Microsoft doesn't call people out of the blue. Ever."

Victor rubbed his temples; he could feel the weight of everything pressing down on him. "I just… I didn't know. He sounded so professional and urgent."

Mia gave him a reassuring pat on the shoulder. "It's not your fault. These scammers are trained to sound convincing. But next time, call me first, okay?"

Victor nodded, but the shame lingered.

The Real Cost of Panic

Tech support scams employ panic and urgency as they prey on trust and fear. For Victor, the cost wasn't just financial it was also emotional. The experience left him wary of legitimate tech support and deeply frustrated with himself for falling for such a simple scam.

These scams don't rely on advanced hacking. They succeed because they exploit human vulnerability, using manipulation and urgency to push victims into making rash decisions.

Lessons for the Rest of Us

Victor's story offers key lessons for avoiding tech support scams:

Unsolicited Calls Are a Red Flag.
Legitimate tech companies don't call customers about system issues. Also, some of these calls might be initiated through a pop up that you clicked, be careful.

Verify the Caller.
Hang up the call, look up the company's official contact number and call them directly to confirm.

Never Grant Remote Access.
Unless you initiate the request, never allow anyone to control your computer.

Consult a Trusted Expert.
If you're unsure, reach out to a tech-savvy friend or family member.

Stay Calm.

Scammers rely on urgency to cloud judgment. Take a moment to assess the situation before acting.

Victor's case was one that was largely based on persuasion using fear as the yardstick to land trust. While he was the victim, this can happen to anyone, especially those who are not tech savvy. The key to ensuring you don't fall victim is to hang up such calls and find someone you trust to help you look into the issue, if any issue really persists. This way, you eliminate the risk of reputational and financial loss.

Chapter 11: The Manipulator's Art

It had been a long day debugging some lines of code that everyone on his team was just looking forward to the end of their day. Kevin leaned back in his chair, suppressing a yawn as he shut down his workstation, ready to call it a day. For him particularly, the day had been long, comprising of back-to-back meetings, an endless list of code reviews, and a last-minute bug that had brought his afternoon to a grinding halt.

As a senior product developer for Trash Technologies, a mid-sized software company specializing in secure payment systems, Kevin was not a stranger to pressure. But then, today was unusually draining. He checked the time, it was 6:27 PM. If he left now, he could catch the 6:45 train from Canary Wharf Station and be home in Stratford by 7:30. Just enough time to grab dinner, crack open a beer, and hop on *Call of Duty* with his multiplayer squad.

He grabbed his backpack without thinking twice and headed for the exit. He was officially done for the day.

The cool evening air greeted him as he stepped onto the bustling streets of London's Canary Wharf business district. Kevin plotted his route home, weaving through the thick crowds of office workers and tourists toward the underground station.

The Mistake

The train was packed as usual. Kevin was lucky to find a corner seat and settled in, resting his bag on his lap. He glanced out the window, his mind wandering as the train pulled away from the platform.

He decided to pass the time by catching up on notifications and chats on his phone. His work emails came first with several messages marked "important," including one about a delay in a critical patch deployment. Kevin opened the email, scrolling quickly through the details, then typed a reply saying "Got it. I'll loop in QA tomorrow."

He switched to checking his social media, liking a few posts from friends and a hiking page he followed on one of the platforms. Then he switched to another platform, where a notification alerted him to a new connection request. All this while, Kevin barely noticed the man sitting next to him, seemingly absorbed in his book but occasionally steering sideways and stealing glances. He had been analyzing Kevin.

The man's gaze drifted to Kevin's ID badge, clipped to his trousers, its text clearly visible…

> Trash Technologies
> Kevin Masters
> Senior Product Developer

The man smirked; his attention now fully fixed on Kevin; he had found his mark.

As the train rocked gently, Kevin opened Codedly, a popular developer app to check the status of a repository update. He scrolled past commit logs and issue trackers, his screen glowing brightly in the carriage. A repository named Trash-PayAPI caught the man's attention. He noted the name and the fact that Kevin appeared distracted, casually flipping between apps.

The Scammer's Perspective

By the time the train reached Stratford, the man already had a plan. He stepped off at the same station as Kevin but made no move to follow him. Instead, he headed for a quiet corner of the platform and launched for his smartphone.

A quick search on one of the social media platforms confirmed Kevin's identity. His public profile listed his role at Trash, his tenure, and a summary of his technical expertise: "Specializing in API development and third-party integrations."

The developer app search, Codedly came next. Kevin's username, tied to his full name, was easy to locate. The good thing was that most of his repositories were private, but their names and public descriptions revealed enough to hint at the projects he was working on. The man felt accomplished for a moment as he discovered a repository that referenced an outdated library known to have vulnerabilities, a detail Trash had yet to address, as evidenced by Kevin's earlier email.

Satisfied by his findings, the man started stoking up ideas within himself. His next move would require precision.

The Friend Request

The following morning, Kevin received a connection request on one of his social networks from "Peter Collins," with a stainless profile that claimed he was a senior technology consultant at a well-known firm. Peter's profile looked legitimate, put together and complete with endorsements and mutual connections. Kevin accepted the request without much thought.

The first message was dispatched within minutes:

"Hi Kevin, I came across your profile while researching payment API systems. Your work at Trash is impressive, I must say! Do you plan to give a presentation at the World Technology conference next month? It would be great to connect with you and exchange ideas."

Kevin replied quickly saying "Thanks, Peter! I appreciate the kind words. I'm not sure if I'll be attending the conference, but it sounds like a great event."

Over the next few days, both men exchanged messages about technology trends, industry challenges and how they both overcome them. Peter, knowing his end game, skillfully steered the conversation toward Trash's work, dropping just enough technical jargon to sound credible.

"I noticed on Codedly, you've been doing some interesting things with third-party authentication," Peter wrote one evening. "That must be very tough to manage, especially with all the vulnerabilities cropping up lately."

Kevin shrugged off his unease. "It's a challenge, but nothing we can't handle. I have a capable team put together that has been working on a patch for some of the issues."

"Good to hear," Peter replied. "You know, if you ever want a fresh perspective, feel free to reach out. I've worked on similar projects and can provide you with insights and guidance."

The Conflict

A few days later, Kevin received an email from Trash's CTO, David Lane. The subject line was urgent, "Critical: Patch Deployment Access."

The email read:

"Kevin,

As the severe vulnerability in the PayAPI system has lingered for too long, Peter Collins has agreed to assist us in addressing the issue. Please provide him with the admin credentials for the beta environment immediately so he can work on a patch. Time is critical.

Thanks,

David."

Kevin frowned. It wasn't unusual for the company to bring in external consultants, but something about the email felt... off, especially since he had recently connected with Peter and had been having conversations with him.

He checked the sender's address: d.lane@Trash-tech.co.uk. It looked legitimate.

Still, Kevin hesitated. He decided to message Peter.

"Hey, Peter—just got an email from our CTO asking me to send you credentials. Can you confirm?"

Peter replied almost immediately. "Absolutely. I'm already in touch with David. He explained to me that this vulnerability could be disastrous if we don't act fast."

Kevin sighed. The urgency in both messages pushed his doubts aside. He forwarded the credentials to the email address provided, feeling a mix of relief and accomplishment.

The Strike

Busy afternoon as usual, Kevin was finishing up his lunch in the breakroom when his phone buzzed with a notification from IT Support.

"Hey, Kevin. Are you running any scripts in the beta environment right now? Seeing unusual activity."

Kevin frowned. He hadn't touched the beta system all morning.

Typing in response, he said…

"Not me. Could it be someone from QA?"

The response came, "Doesn't look like it. Seeing multiple logins from an unrecognized IP."

Kevin's heart skipped a beat. He quickly opened his laptop and logged into the company's admin dashboard. His heart sank as he looked through the activity logs. Several repositories in the beta environment had been accessed and cloned. A few had already been wiped clean.

His phone buzzed again—this time, a call from his manager.

"Kevin," she spoke with a clipped voice, tense from the event. "Who did you give access to the beta system?"

Kevin, now in a confused state, stammered. "I—I sent the credentials to Peter Collins. The CTO said it was urgent. It was for the patch deployment…"

There was a pause at the other end of the line.

"Kevin," she said slowly, "I don't know anyone named Peter Collins. And David Lane would never request credentials over email."

The words hit Kevin like a hammer. He felt a jarring sensation in his head as if he had fallen as he opened the email again. The sender address he thought looked legitimate now seemed glaringly fake- d.lane@Trash-tech.co.uk. It wasn't even the right domain.

"I'll handle it," his manager said sharply. "Get to the war room. Now."

Kevin grabbed his laptop and practically ran to the meeting room where the IT and security teams were gathered. The tension was palpable, the air thick with urgency. They had to begin an incident response process to manage the incident.

"As to the extent of the damage, we know that the attacker cloned and deleted two critical repositories," the head of IT announced. "They also accessed customer API keys and sensitive project documentation. This is a full-blown breach. I believe the intent is to steal as many data as they can."

Kevin sank into a chair, the weight of the situation pressing down on him. "I thought it was real," he murmured, almost to himself.

The head of IT looked at him sternly. "That's exactly what they wanted you to think."

The Aftermath

The aftermath was very brutal. Within hours, news of the breach reached Trash's leadership team. Kevin's actions had compromised not only the beta environment but also client trust. The API keys that Peter accessed in the attack allowed him to initiate fraudulent transactions in sandbox systems, alarming Trash's top customers.

Kevin found himself in several ongoing meetings with his manager, the IT team, and the legal department. Each conversation feeling heavier than the last.

"This isn't entirely your fault, Kevin," his manager said during one meeting, though her tone was strained. "But we need to document exactly how this happened to ensure it doesn't happen again."

Kevin nodded, feeling numb. He knew she was trying to reassure him, but it didn't help. The weight of his mistake crushed him to regret.

That evening, Kevin sat at his desk long after everyone else had gone home, staring blankly at his laptop. He tried to map out how he would have been targeted from his previous activities during the days leading to the attack, he felt he had been profiled. He remembered that he usually wore his ID badge in public, that would have been a start for the perpetrator. He also realized he had a lot of information on his social media accounts that could be pieced by anyone to form a profile on him, his habit of checking his email in public also would have hinted at vulnerabilities. How had he been so blind? Anyone could have been looking over him as he looked at his phone and his laptop in public and crowded places, hence making his private life public.

When he finally made it home, he had lost appetite for food, ignoring the dinner and beer he'd planned and just collapsed onto the couch, too drained to do anything. His phone buzzed with messages from his *Call of Duty* friends wondering where he was, but he just ignored, life had dealt him a bitter pill he needed to recover from.

The breach made headlines the next morning. Trash's reputation took a hit, and customers demanded answers. Kevin's mistake wasn't made public, but internally, he became the unspoken example of what could go wrong when company protocols were ignored.

In the weeks that followed, Trash implemented stricter policies including mandatory phishing training, two-factor authentication for all accounts, and a ban on sharing credentials via email. Kevin knew the changes were necessary, but they felt like a personal indictment. He carried the heaviness for weeks.

"Uncle Kevin are you okay?" his niece asked during a family dinner a month later. Kevin managed to make a weak smile, but the truth was, the bright and energetic Kevin had not felt like himself since the breach.

The Real Cost of Oversharing

Kevin's mistake wasn't malicious, but it was costly. The breach cost Trash financially and reputationally, and it left Kevin grappling with guilt, condemnation and self-doubt. He had always prided himself on being careful and detail-oriented, but the scam had exposed a vulnerability he did not know he had.

Social engineering attacks prey on the very traits that make us human including trust, politeness, and the desire to help. Kevin's experience shows how small, seemingly harmless details can snowball into catastrophic consequences.

Lessons for the Rest of Us

Kevin's story highlights critical lessons about the vulnerabilities we unknowingly create and how scammers can exploit them:

Keep Workplace Details Private.

Wearing an ID badge in public might seem harmless, but it provides valuable information to anyone watching. The company name, your position, and even your name can be enough for scammers to start profiling you. Always secure your badge when you're outside the workplace, tuck it into a bag or pocket to keep it out of sight. Your privacy starts here.

Be Mindful of What You View in Public.

Checking private stuff, work emails, private repositories, or sensitive company information in public spaces like trains or cafes makes it easy for prying eyes to gather details about your activities. You might not notice the person glancing over your shoulder or sitting nearby, but scammers are skilled at watching and remembering key information.

Limit Your Digital Footprint.

Social media and collaboration platforms can unintentionally expose more about you than you realize. Adjust your privacy settings to restrict who can view your profile or make you a connection, and think twice about what you share publicly, especially if it's related to your workplace or ongoing projects.

Verify Before Acting.

If you receive an unusual request for sensitive information, especially from someone claiming to be a superior or external consultant, verify the request through official channels. Call the sender directly or consult your IT team before taking any action.

Trust Your Gut and Pause.

Scammers rely on urgency to cloud your judgment. If a situation feels suspicious, take a moment to pause, think, and verify. That extra second of caution could prevent serious breaches.

Kevin's experience shows us the reason why we need to make privacy a key part of our livelihood. A harmless scroll on social media as much as you think reveals a lot more than we might think. Scammers are skilled at piecing information together to cause harm. The next time you find yourself in public, be mindful of what you view. If you must use your smartphone or laptop, you should invest in a privacy screen.

Chapter 12: When Weak Links Break Chains

Logging the last vendor invoice for the day was Maria's biggest relief. Her head was already pounding from the day's job ensuring the accounts were balanced. The fluorescent lights of Dust Logistics' open-plan office reflecting through her glasses as the once-busy floor now stayed nearly deserted save for herself. She was the company's accountant.

6:53 PM.

Thankful for a very understanding husband, she should have been home over an hour ago, unwinding with a glass of wine in hand. Instead, she had to stay back to close out the tasks for the day that could not be pushed till the next day.

It was the end of a quarter; chaos was expected even with the kind of company she worked with. There were deadlines to meet and numbers to churn to ensure business was running smoothly.

Knowing what the time said, she was almost tempted to push her remaining tasks to the next day. But Maria was meticulous, a good role model for a hardworking staff and her hard work had paid off, earning her promotions, salary bumps and accolades. At the thought of what was at stake, she was not ready to face a cluttered inbox the next day.

With a resigned sigh, she clicked on her inbox. Immediately, she was drawn to one email.

From: HR@DustLogistics-Benefits.com
Subject: Congratulations, Maria! You've Earned a Performance Bonus!

A flicker of excitement pierced through her exhaustion, enough to power her through to complete her tasks. She clicked it open.

The Perfect Trap

The email looked professionally written and polished. It even included the company's logo and a signature from Lisa Carmichael, the HR director. Maria's lips curled into a small smile as she read it.

"Dear Maria,

Your dedication and hard work this quarter have not gone unnoticed and we appreciate all the time and efforts you have put into ensuring the company is on track. We're thrilled to award you a $1,500 bonus. To ensure prompt processing, please confirm your employee ID and credentials by clicking the link below.

Best regards,

Lisa Carmichael

HR Director"

Maria hesitated for only a moment. She had received company-wide emails about phishing scams before, complete with examples of suspicious emails, but this one seemed different.

It wasn't asking for banking information. The link didn't look suspicious as well. Dust Logistics-Benefits.com seemed legitimate. The email was also addressed specifically to her, with details that only someone inside the company would know, as she would assume.

She went ahead and clicked the link, and a familiar-looking portal loaded, asking for her employee credentials. "Easy," Maria murmured as she typed in her username and password: Marias123 / Sunshine89.

The moment she hit *"Submit,"* the page refreshed with a bland error message.

"Session Timed Out. Please Try Again Later."

Maria frowned. "Typical IT issues," as she muttered under her nose, already moving on to her next email so she could finish the day's task. The plan was to get it done the next day.

What Maria didn't realize was that she'd just handed over her credentials to a cloned site.

The Inescapable Countdown

On her way to the office the next morning, brimming with excitement about her bonus, Maria made a quick stop to grab her usual latte as she headed to the office, ready to take on the next day's task. Her face turned pale as she opened the office door and met her boss waiting.

"Maria, we need to talk. Now."

Maria felt confused but had the same expression as Joanna as she followed her to the conference room, wondering if she had missed a task the previous day that would have caused problems only to be met by several members of the IT team who were already gathered there. Their faces were grave, the air in the room heavy with tension.

On the projector screen, a bright red banner flashed ominously.

"UNAUTHORIZED DATA ACCESS DETECTED."

Maria's stomach sank.

Joanna didn't waste time as she cut through the tension. "We've had a major breach; it was traced to a login late last night using your credentials. IT tracked it to someone accessing our internal systems."

Maria felt light-headed immediately, dropping her coffee cup instantly. "What? That's not possible. I didn't—" Her voice, now faint, faltered.

The head of IT, Raj, cut in. "Maria, think carefully. Did you click on any links or enter your credentials anywhere unusual yesterday?"

She immediately remembered the performance bonus email; she felt she had not claimed it since the connection was not successful.

"I…" she stammered. "I got an email from HR about a bonus. It looked real. I thought—"

Raj groaned, running his hand down his face. "It wasn't real. The domain was fake. Did you verify before you clicked? You handed your credentials to an attacker." He was very upset.

Joanna's voice was ice-cold. "Do you understand what your actions have caused? They used your login to access critical systems and now have access to customer records, shipping schedules, and financial reports. Our sensitive data has been compromised. This could cost us millions."

Maria tried to respond but failed to find her words.

The Domino Effect

The breach snowballed into chaos. By midday, the company was receiving multiple calls from clients demanding to know what happened and how they had been affected. Dust Logistics' legal team was in overdrive, drafting statements and planning damage control.

Maria watched it all unfold from the sidelines; she was guilt ridden. The IT team worked furiously to lock down the system and trace the attacker's movements, but the damage was done, and it was severe.

Joanna's words rang in her ears: "This could've been prevented."

The HR team sent out a stern company-wide email that afternoon.

"Reminder: DO NOT enter your credentials on unverified sites. Any suspicious emails should be forwarded to IT immediately."

Though she was not directly named, Maria felt every eye in the office pierce her skin sharply. She avoided the breakroom for the rest of the day, too embarrassed to face her fellow coworkers.

That evening, she sat in her car in the parking lot, staring blankly at the steering wheel. She had spent her entire career building a reputation as dependable and detail oriented. Now, one careless click had changed the narrative.

The Real Cost of Complacency

Maria's mistake wasn't borne from malicious intent, but it exposed a critical vulnerability within Dust Logistics' cybersecurity practices. Despite regular training, she had let exhaustion and routine cloud her judgment, ignoring warning signs that should have been obvious.

The breach didn't just impact the company's finances; it damaged its reputation, strained client relationships, and left Maria grappling with the personal fallout.

Scammers rely on moments of distraction and trust to succeed. Maria's experience is a reminder that cybersecurity isn't just a technical issue, it's a human one. In fact, we are the weakest link in this chain.

Lessons for the Rest of Us

Guard Against Public Exposure.

Be mindful of how and where you access work accounts. Checking emails in public spaces or on unsecured devices increases the risk of breaches.

Verify the Source.

Always scrutinize emails that request credentials or sensitive information, even with personal emails. Check the sender's domain for errors or inconsistencies and verify the request with your IT department when unsure.

Pause Before Clicking.

Scammers count on urgency and excitement to override caution. Think before you act on unexpected offers or requests. You might just be falling for the bait.

Strengthen Your Defenses.

Use unique, strong passwords for all accounts, and update them regularly. Enable two-factor authentication (2FA) for added security.

Don't Ignore the Red Flags.

If something feels off, like an unfamiliar domain name or an unusual request, act on that instinct. Double-check before you proceed. Where you feel really unsure, do not engage.

Maria's actions were not malicious towards the company. In fact, she was loyal to the company because they had treated her right to date. Especially for those of us who work in organizations that do these phishing trainings, even though they may look boring, you should pay attention to them as they teach you about the methods scammers adopt as technology advances to send illegitimate emails that only look to exploit you or your organization. The hook is usually excitement or humanitarian causes. When you get an unfamiliar or unsolicited email or even text message, pause and think. Do not let greed get to you to the point that you click and give out your information. This also goes to websites that we browse, with many popular websites being cloned these days, it is important to be careful to know what website we are interacting with before we share our information.

The Conclusion: Trust, Awareness, and Vigilance

The Digital Battlefield

The internet in its sophistication is both a playground and a battlefield. Every day, billions of people log in to connect, share, learn, and grow, transmitting data in larger quantities than we may even imagine. But lurking in the shadows of this incredible world of possibility are actors who exploit its openness, turning trust into a weapon.

By reading these stories, you can see that the digital age has changed the game. Scams no longer come in plain brown envelopes or shady backroom deals, thieves no longer need to physically point a gun at you for you to surrender your money or belongings. Scams now arrive in polished emails, professional social media messages, and friendly text alerts. Thieves weaponize the internet setting up fake portals and websites that mimic the real thing, using the colors, logos, and language we trust to trick us into opening the door.

Yet, for every scammer, we have a chance to fight back. For every breach, there is a lesson that can help us be better protected. And for every victim, there is an opportunity to turn experience into empowerment.

The stories in this book are not just tales of caution, they are a call to arms and alertness.

The Power of Awareness

Think back to Danielle, who clicked on what she thought was an ordinary email, only to find herself caught in a web of ransomware. Remember Kevin, whose ID badge and digital habits became a puzzle piece in a scammer's master plan.

Consider Maria, whose moment of distraction led to a breach that shook an entire company.

What unites them all is the ordinariness of their actions. They were not reckless people. They were not careless or naive. They were just… human. And this is why these scams are so dangerous, they prey on our very humanity, the fragile emotions that we run on and our hope for better.

But being human also gives us the tools to fight back. With awareness, we can stop scams in their tracks. With vigilance, we can close the gaps that scammers exploit. And with knowledge, we can arm ourselves against even the most sophisticated schemes.

A Challenge for the Reader

This book has shown you the tactics scammers use to infiltrate your world. Now, the challenge is yours.

The next time you receive an email that makes promises that look a little too real or demands an action with urgency, will you pause and think? The next time you're asked for credentials or personal information, will you verify the source? And the next time you see someone else falling for a scam, will you step in to share what you've learned?

Will you share this book?

The internet is a collective space. Our decisions from a click don't just affect us, they ripple outward, impacting our relationships, workplaces, and communities. Your awareness will not just protect you; it will shield those around you.

Beyond This Book

The stories in this book barely scratch the surface of the tactics, schemes, and manipulations that scammers use. As technology evolves, the methods of deception that are used would also evolve. Artificial intelligence-based scams, deepfakes, and ever-more-sophisticated phishing campaigns are already on the rise.

The next book in this series will dive deeper into the cutting-edge threats shaping the future of our cybersecurity. From the dark web marketplaces where stolen data is sold to the psychological tricks that exploit even the most skeptical among us, we'll continue this journey into the heart of the digital underworld.

Imagine being able to recognize a scam before it even takes root. Imagine arming yourself with the skills to not only protect yourself but also help others navigate the treacherous waters of online threats. That's what awaits you in the next installment.

Are you ready to take the next step?

Your Cybersecurity Checklist

Before you close this book, let's recap some steps that will help you secure your digital future.

Guard Your Personal Information.

Be mindful of what you share online, whether it's on social media, job platforms, or even casual emails. Scammers thrive on piecing together seemingly innocuous details. Be mindful of where and how you use your devices also.

Scrutinize Everything.

Never trust an email, message, or call at face value. Verify the source before clicking links, sharing information, or downloading files.

Fortify Your Defenses.

Use strong, unique passwords for every account. Enable two-factor authentication wherever possible.

Stay Informed.

Cybersecurity threats evolve constantly. Keep yourself updated on the latest scams and tactics.

Pause Before Acting.

Urgency is a scammer's best weapon. Take a moment to think before you act. That small pause could save you from big trouble.

A Shared Responsibility

If there's one thing to remember, it's that online safety is not just about protecting yourself, it's about protecting the people and systems you interact with every day. When you verify an email, when you double-check a link, when you strengthen your passwords, you create a ripple of safety that extends far beyond you.

Be the friend who warns others. Be the coworker who advocates for stronger protocols. Be the family member who shares what you've learned.

Need Help? Your Allies in Cybersecurity

The digital world doesn't have to feel like a maze of threats. With the right guidance, it can be a space of opportunity and connection.

If you ever need support navigating cybersecurity challenges, we're here for you. Whether it's personal protection or enterprise-level solutions, our team is dedicated to helping you stay one step ahead.

Follow me and leave a comment on my account and I will connect with you.

Together, we can create a digital future that's safer for everyone.

Final Words

This isn't just a book, it's a movement. A call to arms against the forces that seek to exploit, deceive, and harm. You've taken the first step by arming yourself with knowledge. Now, take the next step by applying it, sharing it, and continuing to learn.

The fight for our cyber safety isn't over. But with every person who chooses awareness over complacency, trust over fear, and vigilance over vulnerability, we move closer to a safer digital future.

See you in the next book.

Appendix: Cybersecurity Terms and Definitions

This appendix provides definitions for some key cybersecurity terms specifically mentioned in this book. Use it as a reference to better understand the threats and concepts discussed.

Authentication: The process of verifying a user's identity before granting access to a system or account. Common methods include passwords, biometrics, or tokens.

Cmd: Command, it is used to open the Command prompt on Microsoft based computers.

FOMO: Fear of Missing Out

GitHub: A widely used platform for hosting and collaborating on code repositories. Public or poorly secured repositories can expose sensitive information.

Malware: Malicious software designed to disrupt, damage, or gain unauthorized access to computer systems. Examples include ransomware and spyware.

Multi-Factor Authentication (MFA): An additional layer of security requiring two or more verification methods to confirm a user's identity.

Phishing: A scam involving deceptive emails or messages that trick individuals into revealing sensitive information, such as login credentials or financial data.

Ransomware: Malware that encrypts a victim's files and demands payment (often in cryptocurrency) to restore access.

SMShing: A form of phishing carried out via text messages, tricking recipients into clicking malicious links or revealing personal information.

Social Engineering: Manipulative tactics used by attackers to exploit trust and convince individuals to divulge confidential information or take harmful actions.

Spyware: Malicious software that secretly gathers information about a user, often used to steal personal data.

Tech Support Scam: A fraudulent scheme where scammers pose as tech support agents to trick victims into granting access to their devices or paying for unnecessary services.

Two-Factor Authentication (2FA): A security process requiring two verification methods, typically a password and a code sent to a mobile device, to secure an account.

Vishing: Voice phishing scams where fraudsters impersonate legitimate organizations during phone calls to extract sensitive information.

VPN (Virtual Private Network): A service that encrypts a user's internet connection, enhancing privacy and security when browsing online.

www.ingramcontent.com/pod-product-compliance
Lightning Source LLC
LaVergne TN
LVHW081529050326
832903LV00025B/1703